A Cup of Encouragement

Inspiring Stories to Fill Your Cup

Wendy Custer

May God Bless You Always!
Wendy Custer

A Cup of Encouragement
Copyright © 2008 by Wendy Custer. All rights reserved.
This book in its entirety – from literary development to artwork and
final design – is a creation of Wendy Custer and may not be reproduced
in any part without written permission from the author.

Photographs on pages 39, 51, and 85 by Randall Beard.

Wendy Custer
28 Covered Bridge Road, Kents Store, VA, 23084
w3vision@hotmail.com

Unless otherwise indicated, all Scripture quotations are taken from the
Holy Bible, New International Version®. Copyright © 1973, 1978,
1984 by the International Bible Society. Used by permission of Zonder-
van Publishing House. All rights reserved.

Scripture taken from THE MESSAGE Copyright © 1993, 1994, 1995,
1996, 2000, 2001, 2002. Used by permission of NavPress Publishing
Group.

Scripture taken from the Living Bible text copyright © 1971 by Tyndale
House Publishers, Wheaton, Illinois.

To my God who equips me:

The Sovereign Lord has given me an instructed tongue,
to know the word that sustains the weary.
He wakens me by morning,
wakens my ear to listen like one being taught.
Isaiah 50:8

To my husband, Jerry, who encourages me:

Thank you for believing in me, supporting me, being patient with me,
and pushing me to accomplish my dreams!

To our children, Carter, Renee, Trevor, and Alden,
and my friends and family who inspire me:

Thank you for the unending supply of stories that you provide me.
Thanks for putting up with me and never giving up on me!

To my Mom, Susan Carter,
and my friend, Heather Perry who help me:

Thank you for your proofreading, advice, and encouragement!

A Cup of Encouragement

2 cups orange drink mix

1 cup sugar

1 cup ice tea mix

¼ cup lemonade mix

Mix all ingredients and store in airtight container to have on hand for any opportunity to warm the body and soul of one in need of encouragement. Add two to three heaping teaspoons to cup of warm water. Serve with a smile, a hug, a listening ear, and a shoulder of comfort. Keep a box of tissues and God's Word available at all times.

Table of Contents

A generous man will prosper;
He who refreshes others will himself be refreshed.
Proverbs 11:25

Therefore encourage one another
and build each other up,
Just as in fact you are doing.
1 Thessalonians 5:11

A Cup of Encouragement

Over the past few years when I have been discouraged, I find myself heading to visit my friend, Heather. We always sit at the kitchen table and chat, and amidst the normal chaos of her life – small children, a million projects, meal preparations, phone ringing, etc. – I always find encouragement. There is a peace, a calm that prevails over and above the mayhem. Without fail when I am low, Heather always makes a cup of her tea and I sip on it while I share my sorrows.

Sometimes she has it on the table before I get there, and sometimes she gets up while we are talking and serves it to me. She never asks whether or not I want it, she just knows I need it. Heather calls it "Russian Tea", some have called it "Friendship Tea," but I would call it "A Cup of Encouragement." It is a rich, hearty tea that warms me to my soul and I find it comforts me when I am sad or cold or empty or even sick to my stomach. It is made from a mixture of several ingredients and Heather keeps it on hand always. She only has to spoon some into a cup and add warm water and it is ready to serve.

I find myself wondering whether we should all have a cup of encouragement ready at any time for those who are discouraged around us. I would like to be a person who could serve up that kind of comfort that warms a cold, empty soul at a moments notice. Often I feel the desire to offer encouragement to someone on the spot but as I search through my cupboard I find that I am out of some of the ingredients that make it so rich. Sometimes the ingredients are there but I haven't prepared them, and by the time I get it all together the opportunity has passed. Sometimes I even find that I have forgotten the recipe.

As God commands us to encourage one another, I believe that He expects us to be ready for the opportunities that come our way. When we are not ready, He will find another who is ready to fill that role. God provides comfort when comfort is needed – I desire to be used by God to comfort others. When *I* fail to be prepared *I* miss the opportunity to be blessed! Let's take the time to be prepared, to learn the ingredients, to stock up on those ingredients, and to know the recipe that provides the comfort for those who need it.

Encourage one another daily, as long as it is called Today,
so that none of you may be hardened by sin's deceitfulness.
Ephesians 3:13

*Stop judging by mere appearances
and make a right judgment.
John 7:24*

*As for those who seemed to be important
– whatever they were makes no difference to me;
God does not judge by external appearance.
Galatians 2:6*

The Bull in My Driveway

I live in a rural area, but I was still surprised when I looked up from weeding the other day to discover two cows in my driveway! They were huge, they were looking right at me, and one of them had horns! Naturally, I assumed the one with horns was a bull (wouldn't you?), and I was scared to death! I quickly put the dogs inside and called a neighbor for help. When he came over, I (with trembling and trepidation) helped him herd the cows into a nearby pasture.

A few other neighbors stopped by and had a good laugh at my expense. They informed me that the correct term for my "bull" was "steer" and, as it turns out, the animal was quite harmless and very gentle. With my limited knowledge of its breeding and background, I had labeled the poor animal based on its appearance. I had judged his whole character from a quick glance.

Recently, two separate individuals from a previous church confessed that they were initially intimidated by my knowledge of Scripture. In the midst of a painful crisis, I had spent hours pouring over the Bible in order to find some comfort. At that time, I was so full of God's Word that it virtually protruded from me! I was excited and eager to share that gift at every opportunity. With limited knowledge of my situation, those who didn't know me labeled me a "know-it-all" and shrank from relationship with me. They judged my character based on the brief encounters we had in Sunday school.

How often do we judge others based on a glance or brief experience? What do we assume about the checkout lady who doesn't look us in the eye or give a friendly greeting? How about the person who runs a red light at the intersection in front of us? How do we judge the new boss who is distant and imposes new and extreme rules? What do we think about the pretty lady with the nice clothes and new car, or the woman who wears the same dress to church every week and drives the piece of junk?

With limited knowledge, we label and judge people incorrectly every day. We must learn to see a person like God sees them. God looks beyond appearances, actions, attitudes, and even words. God looks into the heart to see the true person. We must take the time to get to know a person - find out what it is that causes their anger, or sadness, or empty smile. Find out where a person comes from, or where they are now. We all have a story, a background, and all of our experiences add up to make us who we are. We all have something to give and need something from each other. When we judge someone on their appearance or a brief encounter, we are likely to miss out on valuable relationships.

Take the time this week to find out something about the "bull" in your driveway. Don't shrink from those who seem intimidating or different. Pray about how you can get to know the true person under the horns. You may be surprised when they turn out to be a totally harmless and gentle animal!

The Lord does not look at the things man looks at.
Man looks at the outward appearance, but the Lord looks at the heart.
1 Samuel 16:7b

Yet he did not waver through unbelief
regarding the promise of God,
but was strengthened in his faith
and gave glory to God,
being fully persuaded that God had
the power to do what he had promised.
Romans 4:20-21

"For my thoughts are not your thoughts,
neither are your ways my ways,"
declares the Lord.
"As the heavens are higher than the earth,
so are my ways higher than your ways and my
thoughts than your thoughts."
Isaiah 55:8-9

God's Promise

How much faith do we truly put in God's promises? Once, God gave me an opportunity to experience what I sound like when I question Him.

Carter's Dad usually took him to Boy scouts. One week however since he had a prior commitment, I was to fill in. I knew the meeting was at 7:00, but I had an important delivery to make on the way, so we left early. "But Mom," Carter complained, "We never leave this early!" I explained that I had something else important to do, but that we would still be at the meeting on time. As soon as we pulled out of the driveway, Carter began to worry.

"This isn't the way we go!"

"I know that, but remember, I have something else to do first. I will get you there!"

"We're going to be late!"

"Trust me, I planned for this! I will get you there!"

"Are you sure you know how to get there? Are you sure we won't be late? Are you sure it is the right night? What time is it? Are we almost there?"

Finally, I was fed up with his worrying. "Carter", I said *very* sharply, "Why can't you trust me? Didn't I promise you that we would get there on time?" Just then a very quiet voice said, *"Wendy, you do this to Me all of the time."*

So often I question God on His timing and His plan. Even when I have clearly heard Him promise me something, I get tired of waiting. I don't understand the way He goes about things and frankly sometimes it seems as though He has forgotten. Instead, it is I that have forgotten that God's ways are not my ways and His thoughts are not my thoughts (Isaiah 55:8). Just as I had something else important to accomplish on the way to Carter's event, God has many important things to accomplish along the way. Just as I had planned ahead to make it all work together, God has it all planned out as well. In Jeremiah 29:11, God explains to His people that He has not forgotten about them and that He intends to fulfill His promise in His time.

"For I know the plans I have for you," declares the Lord, "plans to prosper you and not to harm you, plans to give you a hope and a future."

I am not so unlike Carter. I worry about things that I don't understand, I lack patience, and I ask a lot of questions. Though God has never let me down, I am still learning to trust Him. Here is a verse that He gave me lately to help me remember. I hope that you will read it and embed it in your heart for those times when you find yourself saying, "God, are we there yet?"

The Lord is not slow in keeping His promise, as some understand slowness.
He is patient with you, not wanting anyone to perish,
but everyone to come to repentance.
2 Peter 3:9

6

All of this I have spoken while still with you.
But the Counselor, the Holy Spirit,
whom the Father will send in my name
will teach you all things
and will remind you of everything I have said to you.
John 14:25-26

So I will always remind you of these things, even though you know
them and are firmly established in the truth you now have. I think it is
right to refresh your memory as long as I live in the tent of this body,
because I know that I will soon put it aside, as our Lord Jesus Christ
has made clear to me. And I will make every effort to see that after
my departure you will always be able to remember these things.
2 Peter 1:12-15

A Reminder

There are days that I forget what my God has done for me. On those days, I am typically feeling sorry for myself, or lost and confused about my direction in life. I sometimes decide to go my own way and follow my own plans, even though they result in devastation. It seems that I forget who I am and who my Father is! Though He carried me yesterday, today I do not remember.

I have been thinking a lot lately about short term memory loss. We recently watched a movie called Fifty First Dates. In this movie, a girl has been in an accident and sustained a brain injury that erased her short term memory. Every night, as she sleeps, her brain erases the day before and she is unable to remember anything since the accident.

One day a man comes into the restaurant where she is having breakfast. When they meet, he is fascinated by her and they spend the whole morning together. He falls in love with her and her with him, but that night as she sleeps, she forgets him. For the next fifty days, he meets her and woos her in a new way each day, even knowing that she won't remember him. Eventually, he comes up with the idea to make a video tape for her to view each morning when she wakes, to remind her of her life, who she is, how much he loves her, and even that she loves him.

I love to think of our God in that way. We have such short term memory loss. We forget how much our God loves us. We forget that we belong to Him. We forget the blessings that he has heaped on us, and how He has carried us through the hard times. Most importantly, we forget the sacrifice of His Son for us.

Thank God that He loves us enough to continue to woo us, even when we forget Him. He has new mercies for us each morning and He has new ways to pursue us each day. He never gives up and always searches for us! No matter how far we go, or how little we think of Him each day, He constantly has His eye on us.

God has a reminder for us as well, in His word. He has written a book for us to remind us of the story of how he has pursued us and made plans for our lives with Him. If we rise each morning, read His love letter to us, and spend time in His presence then we will be reminded of who we are in Christ, who He is, how much He loves us, and even that we love Him!

We, in our human minds, do have a short term memory loss. We focus so much on today that we forget what He did for us yesterday. But God promises to continue to remind us. We may forget, but He will never forget! Once we belong to Him, we will always belong to Him!

I will remember the deeds of the LORD; yes, I will remember your miracles of long ago.
I will meditate on all your works and consider all your mighty deeds.
Psalm 77:11-12

God is our refuge and strength,
an ever-present help in time of trouble.
Psalm 46:1

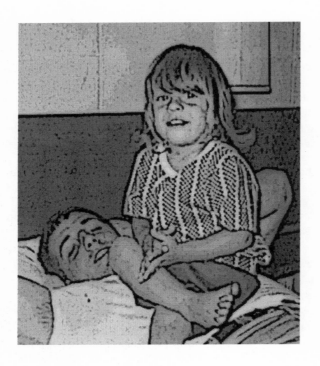

"Because he loves me," says the Lord, "I will rescue him;
I will protect him, for he acknowledges my name.
He will call upon me, and I will answer him;
I will be with him in trouble, I will deliver him and honor him.
With long life will I satisfy him and show him my salvation."
Psalm 91:15-16

Daddy

When I opened my first checking account, I had a hard time keeping up with my finances. There should be some kind of a test you have to pass in order to be given an ATM card, however they gave me one and I was not afraid to use it! It wasn't long before I had bounced several checks. This was way before the days of online banking, so it was a while before I realized that I had over drafted my account. Before I knew what had happened, I had so many returned check fees that I couldn't figure out how to get out of the hole. I tried to call the bank and handle it myself, but all that they could tell me was that everyday that I didn't take care of my debt, the total would get bigger. I felt completely confused and helpless – so, I called my daddy! Dad called the bank manager and I am not sure what he said to that man, but somehow the fees got reduced and I got back on track.

There have been many times in my life where the circumstances where bigger than what I could handle. Whether I had made a mistake, or I was being treated unfairly, I knew I could count on my dad to help me figure out a way to handle it. He had the authority, the resources, and the ability to be able to deal with things I couldn't. Unfortunately as life has gone on, I have come to realize that there are things in my life that even my daddy doesn't have the resources to handle. However, my Heavenly Father has unlimited resources!

Like my dad, God is pleased when I am strong. He wants me to learn to be grown up and to do the things He has taught me to do. But there is no daddy in the world, including my Heavenly Father that doesn't love to have his little girl come running to him. God is delighted when we realize that we need Him. He is waiting to use His authority, resources, and abilities to help us in time of need. He may not rescue us from every situation, but He will walk through each of them with us and we can be sure that we have His protection.

My dad was not pleased with my lack of banking ability. He did not let the opportunity slip by to educate me on the use of an ATM card and the importance of recording my transactions. He also did not excuse me from paying the fees that were left. His discipline was an important growth step for me and I have not forgotten it. Maybe my dad forgot it though, because he never mentioned it again. Even when I have made other mistakes, he didn't bring it up. You see, Dad forgave me. I came to him with a repentant heart and a humble attitude and though I still had to face the consequences, in his eyes it was done.

What a picture of grace! God waits for us to come to Him in humility and repentance. He will often use the circumstances as a time for discipline and instruction, but He also forgives us and He never brings it up again! Whatever is going on in your life today, don't forget that your Abba, your Daddy, your Heavenly Father is ready and waiting. He has the authority, the resources, the ability, the time, and the desire to help you with whatever you need. Nothing is too big for Him!

The Lord is compassionate and gracious, slow to anger, abounding in love.
He will not always accuse, nor will he harbor his anger forever;
He does not treat us as our sins deserve or repay us according to our iniquities.
For as high as the heavens are above the earth, so great is his love for those who fear him;
As far as the east is from the west, so far has he removed our transgressions from us.
As a father has compassion on his children,
so the Lord has compassion on those who fear him.
Psalm 103: 8-13

10

Do not conform any longer
to the pattern of this world,
but be transformed by the
renewing of your mind.
Romans 12:2

You were taught,
with regard to your former way of life,
to put off your old self,
which is being corrupted by its deceitful desires;
to be made new in the attitude of your minds;
and to put on the new self,
created to be like God in true righteousness and holiness.
Ephesians 4:22-24

Transformation

A couple of weeks ago, my two year old, Trevor, spied a green caterpillar climbing up the tree in our yard. We decided to catch him and put him in Trev's bug keeper so we could show Carter when he got home from school. It was a Wednesday, and Trevor was so pleased with his caterpillar that he even brought him to church that evening, and the bug keeper sat on his nightstand as he slept. The next morning, however, Trevor could not see his caterpillar. Hanging from the top of his bug keeper was a green sack. His caterpillar was in a cocoon. We read stories about caterpillars and talked about how God changes them to butterflies and Trev was content to check on the cocoon each day. We really didn't know how long it would take but we were prepared to wait as the caterpillar was transformed. One week later after the boys were in bed, Trevor came running out of his room. "My caterpillar changed into a butterfly!" He exclaimed. We all went outside and watched our little friend take his first flight! What an exciting experience!

I have to wonder about the caterpillar and how much he must be like us. Does he crawl along on his belly wondering about his purpose? Does he think that his life will always be this way – after all, this is how he was made – or do you think he knows that he will someday have beautiful wings to help him soar? Does he know that he will never have to crawl again? How do you think he feels when he is stuck in that cocoon for days, or weeks, or months? Does he feel trapped, claustrophobic, imprisoned? When his wings begin to grow inside that cocoon, is it painful? Does he wish he could go back to crawling and munching leaves? How does he feel the first time he stretches his wings? How scary it must be the first time he lifts off the ground! How exhilarating to take that first flight, to see how high he can go, to flutter effortlessly to the top of a tree, a trip that before would have taken him days. Do you think he feels that his days of confinement and pain were worth the outcome? Do you think he praises God for his transformation?

I think we can learn much from our little caterpillar friend. How many of us are content to crawl along and munch the leaves we can reach without realizing that our purpose is much, much more. There are three steps in transformation, the change that God desires in us. We must change in order to become more like Christ. The first step is that we must <u>want</u> to change. Philippians 2:13 says, *God is working in you giving you the desire to obey Him and the power to do what pleases Him.* Once the spirit convicts us and we have that desire to change, the next step requires an action from us. We must then <u>decide</u> to change. Ephesians 4:23 says *to be made new in the attitude of your mind.* By immersing ourselves in God's Word and praying for His truths, we allow the truth to take root in our minds. The third step is to make the <u>effort</u> to change, this is obedience. 1 John 5:3 says, *"This is love for God: to obey His commands."*

Just as a lowly caterpillar is transformed into a glorious butterfly, I want to be transformed into His likeness!

And we, who with unveiled faces all reflect the Lord's glory, are being transformed into his likeness with ever-increasing glory, which comes from the Lord, who is the Spirit.
2 Corinthians 3:18

Then the righteous will shine like the sun
in the kingdom of their Father.
Matthew 13:43

And we have the word of the prophets
made more certain,
and you will do well to pay attention to it, as to a
light shining in a dark place,
until the day dawns and the morning star
rises in your hearts.
2 Peter 1:19

Sonshine

Many years ago for a period of time, it rained for what seemed like weeks and weeks. Each day seemed gloomier than the last and we thought that the sun would never shine again. I stopped by one of the children's school one day during that dreary time and as I stepped in the door and shook out my umbrella, I was met by one of the teachers.

"Well hello Wendy," she exclaimed. *"Did you bring the sun with you today?"*

Her question stopped me dead in my tracks! While I knew in my head that she was asking if I brought the S U N, the Holy Spirit was asking in my heart if I had brought the S O N. That simple question on a rainy day has changed my life!

If I am going to proclaim to have Jesus in my heart, then I must be willing to take Him with me everywhere I go. If He is with me wherever I go, then I must also be willing to let the world see Him in me. How will anyone know that Jesus lives within me unless I go about my day with a spirit of Joy, Peace, and Love?

It may not be the rainy season where you live right now. Maybe the sun is shining brightly in your neck of the woods, but you can be certain that someone who will cross your path today is living a dreary life. People all around us are in despair and sinking into a black hole of depression. There are those you will meet who are facing weeks of gloominess because of the pain of broken relationships, sickness, and financial devastation. Some people have a life that seems devoid of hope and full of the disappointment of lost dreams. They look around them and wonder when the clouds will lift and the sun will shine again.

When we come across these people, they will look to see, "Did you bring the Son with you today?" We may be the only glimmer of hope that they will see. We could be the only one that provides them with the encouragement they need to make it through one more day. The smile on our face, the warm words that we use, the patience that we display, the kindness that we offer, these are the ways that we let the Son penetrate their darkness.

Wherever we go, whatever we do, regardless of our own circumstances, we must be willing to take the Son with us. We must let Him shine through us to all who desperately need Him. So, how about you? "Did you bring the Son with you today?"

A cheerful heart is good medicine,
but a crushed spirit dries up the bones.
Proverbs 17:22

You have made known to me the path of life.
Psalm 16:11

But small is the gate and narrow the road
that leads to life, and only a few find it.
Matthew 7:14

The Line

I spent time in the woods today, seeking God's voice – His wisdom for this leg of my journey. He spoke, but it was not the direction I was expecting.

I left my backpack in the tree stand and headed for the creek. Many times God has spoken to me there. The sound of the running water is restorative to my soul. It was my goal to get there, as I knew that was where I would hear Him. But He had other plans.

As I set out, I followed a small creek running through the woods. I love that little creek, it is full of twists and turns and tiny falls. I knew that eventually it would lead me to the big creek I was seeking. After a while though, I came to a boundary line and I recognized that I would have to turn away from the little creek and walk along the line until I came to my destination. I knew I could just keep going through the other property and I may reach the creek faster, but it was hunting season and it would be dangerous, not to mention wrong.

I noticed, as I followed the boundary line, that it was clearly marked. If I were to cross into the other land and I were caught – there would be no excuse. I knew what the markers meant. There was no fence to keep me out, no guards to enforce the rule, just the signs and warnings and my own knowledge of the truth.

A few times in my walk, the signs were not as clear. There were some that were missing or spaced too far apart, but I had been walking the boundary for long enough to know that I must search for the markers and not let that be an excuse for crossing the line.

Several times I felt cold, impatient, and anxious, and I was tempted to cut through and cross the line, but I was reminded that shortcuts are not the wise way. The way of the Lord is straight and narrow. He will get us to the promised destination, but it will be in His way and His timing.

Eventually, I reached the creek. I sat quiet and still ready to hear God's Word for me. The message was clear, "Your lesson was in the journey, not the destination."

Let your eyes look straight ahead, fix your gaze directly before you.
Make level paths for your feet and take only ways that are firm.
Do not swerve to the right or the left; keep your foot from evil.
Proverbs 4: 25-27

*This water symbolizes baptism that now saves you
also - not the removal of dirt from the body
but the pledge of a good conscience toward God.
It saves you by the resurrection of Jesus Christ.*
1 Peter 3:21

*Let us draw near to God with a sincere heart
in full assurance of faith,
having our hearts sprinkled to cleanse us
from a guilty conscience
and having our bodies washed with pure water.*
Hebrews 10:22

Messy Souls

In the children's bathroom in our home, there is a white rug. Often, after the kid's nightly showers, I find muddy footprints on that rug, a telltale sign of where they have been during the day. They do a great job of scrubbing the rest of their little bodies, ridding themselves of the dirt and grime from their many activities, but they sometimes forget to wash their feet. Though the children may look and smell clean, they track the evidence of their messy soles for all to see.

What tracks do your footprints leave? Life is messy, but most of us do a pretty good job of scrubbing ourselves up, removing the grime of the day. We take deep sighs, count to ten, listen to soothing music, and maybe even take long baths. Some of us read novels, go for a long run, drink green tea or maybe something a little stronger. These things are not necessarily bad; finding healthy ways for dealing with stress is good. We have many tools for ridding us of the dirt on our souls. However hard we try though, a residue will remain and when we step back out into the world, our tracks will show the truth.

Just as our children's feet get dirty in the regular play of everyday, we also get dirty. Whether it is mistakes that we make, disappointments of life, difficult circumstances, or broken relationships, life is hard. We carry those disappointments and difficulties with us throughout the day, leaving dirt and grime on our souls. The heaviness that we feel at the end of the day is the result that stress takes on our soul. When we rest our bodies and ease our minds, but don't take care of our souls we are only partially clean.

During the last supper, Jesus took on the job of a servant and washed the feet of the disciples. His act was a symbol of how we should serve one another, but I think we can take something else from this as well. Each day brings troubles and concerns and we cannot be effective if we carry those troubles into the next day. Jesus Himself will wash the dust of the day from our feet if we allow Him. No matter what we try in our lives to clean up our souls, Jesus is the only one who can get us truly clean. When we take our day to Him - when we release the dirt and grime of our mistakes, our hurts, and our circumstances, He will clean our feet. He will wash away the dust and give us a fresh start. When we walk across the room after spending time with the Lord, we will no longer track the evidence of our messy souls for all to see.

Cleanse me with hyssop, and I will be clean;
wash me and I will be whiter than snow.

*Through patience a ruler can be persuaded,
and a gentle tongue can break a bone.
Proverbs 25:15*

*For the kingdom of God is not
a matter of talk but of power.
What do you prefer?
Shall I come to you with a whip
or in love and with a gentle spirit?
1 Corinthians 4:21*

Broken by Gentleness

    I once heard a story of a strong boulder that was broken into pieces, not by force but by gentleness.

    In a rock quarry, the strong, young men pounded away at a boulder. With brute force they swung the sledge hammers against the rock over and over in an attempt to break it apart. But it was to no avail, for the rock refused to be broken. No strength it seemed was strong enough; no amount of striking would weaken its hardness. Finally, in desperation, they called over the foreman. The quiet old man examined the rock. It seemed an impossible task since the beating from the younger men had not even caused it to chip. But the old man quietly reached into his back pocket and withdrew a whisk broom. Slowly, carefully, he swept away all of the dust and dirt from the surface. After it was swept clean the man bent down close and with his fingers searched every inch. His discerning eye spied a small crack, a vein, barely visible. He placed a chisel against the crack and tapped gently with a small hammer. In amazement the strong young men watched as the boulder crumbled before their eyes.

    Let us remember that it does not take hammering and pounding to crack open the difficult relationships in our life. Instead let us rely on the tenderness and wisdom of God. We must use the power of prayer and forgiveness to sweep clean the dusty surface of those relationships. Then with patience and love we can examine them for cracks. With a gentle hand and a kind heart we can tap away with God's truth until the shell crumbles.

Tremble, O earth, at the presence of the Lord,
at the presence of the God of Jacob,
who turned the rock into a pool,
the hard rock into springs of water.
Psalm 114: 7-8

I run in the path of your commands,
for you have set my heart free.
Psalm 119:32

The mind of sinful man is death,
but the mind controlled by the Spirit
is life and peace.
Romans 8:6

Anticipation

My husband, Jerry, surprised me the other day by borrowing a motorcycle and taking me for my first ride. I was a little apprehensive in the beginning, so I held on tightly, frightened that I might fall off. Once I relaxed the feeling of the wind rushing by me and the beauty of the scenery was delightful! What I enjoyed most, however, really took me by surprise.

As a woman, I like to be in control - even when it is a false sense of control. When I ride in the passenger seat of a car, I am always watching to see what is ahead. I try to anticipate what might happen; obstacles in the road, people pulling out in front of us, curves in the road, etc. I am constantly using my passenger side brake, putting my hands on the dashboard, gripping the door handle tightly, and even giving advice. Though Jerry may actually be driving, I worry about our safety and sometimes even doubt his skill.

As I sat behind Jerry on the motorcycle, though, his helmet blocked my view from the front. I couldn't see what was coming or where we were going. With the wind and the sound of the engine, I couldn't talk with him about which way to go or even how long we were planning to ride. Each time we stopped, I fully participated in whatever there was to do, but I had no say in the how, when, or even why we got there. The journey was up to Jerry - I was just along to enjoy the ride. I found joyous freedom in that lack of control!

In life, what kind of passenger are you? Do you assume that you are in charge and try to make things happen by applying your imaginary brake or giving advice to God on the direction you think life should go? We don't need to say "Jesus, take the wheel!" He already has it! God is in control, we only need to recognize that and relinquish our feeble attempts to take over. Whenever we pretend to be the authority, we miss the opportunity to enjoy the journey and we disturb the peace for everyone around.

Instead, we should take a seat behind our Lord, trusting Him to give us the ride of our life! With God as the head, we have the protection and shelter that we need. We no longer need to try to anticipate the obstacles ahead. Though there will be bumps in the road, He's got it all under control! We should hold on to Him and prepare ourselves for the next stop along the road. When we get to where we are going, we can fully participate in that event instead of spending our energy worrying about how, when, or even why we got there.

What freedom there is to experience out there on the open road with the wind in our hair and no need to anticipate the future! Relax, hold on, and enjoy the ride!

May the God of hope fill you with all joy and peace as you trust in Him, so that
you may overflow with hope by the power of the Holy Spirit.
Romans 15:13

Now finish the work, so that your eager willingness
to do it may be matched by your completion of it,
according to your means.
2 Corinthians 8:11

However, I consider my life worth nothing to me,
if only I may finish the race and complete the task
the Lord Jesus has given me – the task of testifying
to the gospel of God's grace.
Acts 20:24

I'm Done!

As I was waiting for Trevor's class to come outside the other day, I watched another teacher begin her students on a project. She had given each one of them some sidewalk chalk and assigned them to a square of concrete along the edge of the playground. They began enthusiastically, but it was only a few moments before some of the children lost their interest in the work. She encouraged them one by one to work some more, but she quickly became overwhelmed by the repeated comment, "I'm done!" Her response was one I, myself, have given, but it took me off guard as I felt convicted with my own short attention span!

"There is no done," she said. "You must fill up your whole square!" As a former elementary art teacher, those words rang in my ears. Children will often draw a small picture in the middle of a large sheet of plain white paper. They are perfectly happy with their accomplishment and usually see no need to do any more. A good composition, however, is a balanced and full picture. A large amount of white space left over leaves the viewer with an empty, uncomfortable feeling that something is unfinished. As an instructor, I always encouraged my students to add more, to keep working, to use their space and their time wisely.

I often find myself saying "I'm done!" Life is complicated and I have been assigned to some things that are rather difficult. Sometimes I am tired of relationships that take a lot of work. I am often frustrated with projects that don't seem exciting and rewarding. I can get bent out of shape when I don't know where to go next, or when I am out of my comfort zone. There are many times when I have no idea why I should bother to continue with something or someone. But God says, "There is no done! You must fill up your square."

We are all assigned to difficult things: difficult relationships, difficult jobs, difficult health issues, difficult children. We usually don't mind making a stroke or two, but how long does it take before we are "done"? We live in a society that does not encourage sacrifice. We are taught to live for the moment, and if we don't like the moment then - move on. We are not unlike our children who want to be constantly entertained. We do not like discomfort and we expect to be happy all of the time.

God, however, has not promised us constant happiness. He is much more interested in developing our character. But He has promised us hope, joy, peace and many other things. Most of these promises come about when we have learned lessons from experience. We learn hope when we are in need. We learn joy when we are in pain. We learn peace when we are surrounded by chaos. If we fail to experience these things because we are "done" before the assignment is complete, it is like an unfinished painting or a blank white sheet.

It takes work to complete something, perseverance to keep on going, and diligence to not give up! But when we don't give up, when we keep going, when we complete the assignment, the outcome is amazing! Our lives can be full, complete, balanced compositions, instead of just a little scribble here and there. Are you "done"? Take a step back and review the assignment. Look at the big picture with fresh eyes. Dig deep, ask for help, and get creative. Above all, don't give up! The rewards for filling up your whole square are more than you can ever imagine.

Let us not become weary in doing good,
For at the proper time we will reap a harvest if we do not give up.
Galatians 6:9

Let the word of Christ dwell in you richly
as you teach and admonish one
another with all wisdom.
Colossians 3:16

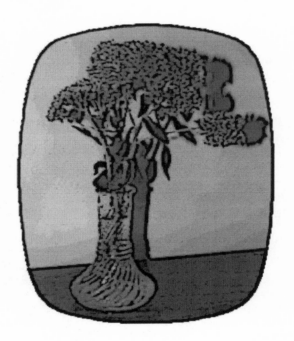

I seek you with all my heart;
do not let me stray from your commands.
I have hidden your word in my heart
that I might not sin against you.
Psalm 119:10-11

Immersed In Truth

Have you ever seen the experiment where you put a white carnation into a glass of colored water? Over time the stem of the carnation draws the water into itself. It is immersed in the water and uses it for nourishment. Therefore, whatever is in the water is also consumed. After a period of time the water reaches the flower and whatever color the water was, the white flower becomes. The flower doesn't change, but it takes on the color of the water. The flower is merely a container or a form for the color.

We are very much like a carnation. We are colored by what we take in. If we immerse ourselves in God's word, His truth will seep into our lives. That truth will begin to show through us in our actions and we will live out his truth because our thoughts will be those of Christ. However, if we immerse ourselves in other things, we will be colored by them as well. If we are immersed in the lies of the world, we will become like the world. If we are immersed in unforgiveness or self-pity, we will take on the color of those things. If we become immersed in business, legalism, apathy, or complacency, then those are the colors that we will become.

Many of us feel that we are exposed to God's truth enough to do the trick. But is simply being exposed to the truth enough? If we lay the carnation on the table next to the glass of colored water, will it take on the color of the water? If we dip the stem into the water occasionally but then remove it, will it become that color? Suppose we sprinkle some of the colored water onto the flower, does the flower then change color? Of course, we know that these things will not change the flower. The only way to truly change it is to immerse it and leave it there.

Where is your Bible? It is not enough for it to be in the same room with you. It is not enough to hear it on Sunday Morning. It is not enough to read an inspirational email. God's truth is amazing. His Word is living and powerful. However, the only way for us to truly change, to become more like Christ, and to be living examples of His truth, is to be immersed in His Word and to stay there. His word can seep through us to change ashes to beauty, pain to joy, chaos to peace, and bitterness to love. Immerse yourself and allow Him to color your life.

If you remain in me and my words remain in you,
ask whatever you wish and it will be given to you.
This is to my Father's glory, that you bear much fruit,
showing yourselves to be my disciples.
John 15:7-8

26

Laziness lets the roof leak,
and soon the rafters begin to rot.
Ecclesiastes 10:18

Therefore, if you are offering your gift at the alter
and there remember that your brother has
something against you,
leave you gift there in front of the alter.
First go and be reconciled to your brother;
then come and offer your gift.
Matthew 5:23-24

We Have a Leak!

"We have a leak!" came the frantic cry from the basement. Down the steps we raced in hopes that we could catch the plumbing problem before it became a big issue, but we were too late! A huge bulge in the ceiling and a growing dark spot were the proof that this condition had existed unnoticed for quite some time. Now, the small drip that came from the ceiling was just a symptom of a big problem. After some investigating, we discovered that the leak originated with a tiny hole in the tube that carried water to our icemaker in the kitchen upstairs. That little hole had released a steady steam of water for a long time which in turn filled up the ceiling in the den below. After a while, the ceiling could no longer hold the water and it began to give. When the problem was finally detected the damage was astronomical.

There have been many times in my relationships when a small issue became almost irreparable. Often there is a "hole" in our communication that causes a small, steady leak. Left unattended it can fill up the relationship with emotions and cause a strain that grows and grows. If the problem goes unnoticed, we could be faced with such damage that it may seem impossible to repair.

Such a "hole" could be caused by the sharpness of our words. Something we say or do could pierce the spirit of a loved one causing them to feel unloved or injured. Without repairing the damage, their hurt can become anger, anger can become unforgiveness, unforgiveness can lead to bitterness, and on it goes.

Other "holes" in our communication may come from the lack of something said. If we are not sure that our communication is complete, we leave room for misunderstanding. Misunderstanding opens the way to assumption, assumption makes room for hurt feelings, and the cycle begins again. The enemy needs only a small crack to begin a steady stream of deception!

We must make sure that we are patching these holes before they become a huge problem. It is much simpler and less painful to repair a small hole in a tube than to replace an entire ceiling. In the same way, it is better to apologize for a small offense or oversight than to restore a relationship full of resentment and bitterness. The Bible tells us that if we remember that we have an issue with someone, we are to go immediately to that person to work it out (Matthew 5:23-34). We are not to let that small thing turn into something huge.

Let us keep a close eye on our relationships so that there will be no frantic cry that "we have a leak!"

See to it that no one misses the grace of God
and that no bitter root grows up to cause trouble and defile many.
Hebrews 12:15

When God created man,
He made him in the likeness of God.
Genesis 5:1

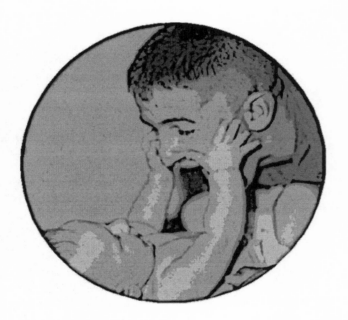

Do not conform any longer to the pattern of this world,
but be transformed by the renewing of your mind.
Romans 12:2

An Unmistakable Likeness

When my son Carter, was a baby, his Uncle Devin lived with us. Devin is crazy about kids and takes his role as an uncle very seriously! He spent hours playing with Carter, teaching him new things, and of course, spoiling him. One of their favorite games was when Devin would put Carter on the floor and lean his face right over top of him. Devin would make faces at Carter and talk to him and Carter would play with Devin's face and pull on his ears. They were a funny pair!

Carter is now eleven years old. It has been ten years since his uncle was a daily part of his life; however, I see Devin's expressions on Carter's face all the time. Carter does resemble Devin somewhat in his stature and features, but it is the way he moves his eyes and mouth, the way he speaks, and even the way he walks that is so familiar. Sometimes it just blows me away how much he looks like Uncle Devin!

I am certain that genetics play a part in those familiar ways, but I am convinced that it was Carter's exposure to Devin during those early months that cemented his likeness into Carter forever. As he was learning how to make expressions and movements, he was learning to do them Devin's way.

Likewise, when we spend time with the Lord, we too begin to look like Him. As we read His word and talk with Him, we take on His ways. The more time we spend with Him, the more we will resemble Him!

Just as Carter got some of Devin's resemblance from the family line, we get some of our godliness from our family line. The Bible tells us that we are created in God's image, so it is expected that we will look something like Him. However, it is in the daily time that we spend only with Him that creates an unmistakable likeness to our Lord. When we turn our eyes upon Him and look fully in His face, when we block out the rest of the world and make Him our focus, it is then that we are being transformed.

Carter is so proud when we tell him that he looks like Uncle Devin! We should also look forward to the day when someone compliments us on our likeness to the Lord. We should desire with all our hearts to have His expressions of love and peace imprinted on our lives so that we may reflect His image to all who see us.

We can be mirrors that brightly reflect the glory of the Lord.
And as the Spirit of the Lord works within us,
we become more and more like Him.
2 Corinthians 3:18

A heart at peace gives life to the body,
but envy rots the bones.
Proverbs 14:30

Better a dry crust with peace and quiet
than a house full of feasting with strife.
Proverbs 17:1

He who covers an offense promotes love,
but whoever repeats the matter
separates close friends.
Proverbs 17:9

A man's wisdom gives him patience;
it is to his glory to overlook an offense.
Proverbs 19:11

Cat and Mouse

My cats have a cat door so that they can come and go as they please. It is nice for them so that they can be indoors or outdoors at their whim, and it is nice for me because I do not have to fool with a litter box. They are great hunters though, and sometimes they bring their prey indoors. Often, when they bring in a mouse it is still alive and they enjoy playing with it. The cat will knock the poor little mouse around, batting it to and fro with his paws. Usually, he doesn't even plan on eating it and he definitely isn't planning to let it go - he just wants to play. Eventually, half dead, the mouse sneaks away and hides under something, like my stove or the sofa, and dies. After a few days, the mouse begins to stink! It is amazing how something as small as a dead mouse can have such a bad odor!

As nasty as all of this seems, we have a tendency to do the same thing with our troubles. We bring them indoors into the midst of our lives and relationships. With no intention to "let it go", we play with them, knocking our problems about back and forth. Most of the time our issues roll up under the stuff of our everyday lives, half dead and stinking to high heaven. Though the trouble may have been trivial in the beginning, the odor of the dead issue can be smelled by all who come around! Do you have an odor in your life? There are three steps to take to assure that your life and your relationships have a sweet aroma; get rid of the stink, remove the cat door, and conquer the troubles as they come, disposing of the carcass immediately!

The first step will require a little elbow grease! Follow your nose to find the smell. Look under the normal everyday things and the closest of your relationships. Examine the things that have happened recently and not so recently. Once you discover the source of the smell, put on some gloves and get it out of there! Prayer, trusted friends, and godly counsel are useful tools for exterminating! It may take a little while for the odor to disappear, but without the rotting carcass, the air will soon clear out!

Second - don't bring your troubles indoors! When something happens that hurts you, keep it out of your other relationships and your everyday functioning. Having a troublesome issue darting about, does only harm and not good. Distraction and even disease can follow, leading to the destruction of the things you hold most dear. Find a safe place outside to deal with your stuff. If you need help, invite someone out there to join you in the effort.

Thirdly, conquer and destroy! Beating a dead horse has never been effective, and a dead mouse is no better. If you have an issue to deal with, sooner is better. Put your focus on getting it done and then be done with it! Troubles do come and when they do, they disrupt everything. When we deal with them promptly, we can get back to our lives and our relationships. Take the clothespin off of your nose and go deal with your stench! Everyone in your life will be relieved and you can go on living life as usual!

The troubles of my heart have multiplied; free me from my anguish.
Psalm 25:17

We also rejoice in our sufferings,
because we know that
suffering produces perseverance;
perseverance, character;
and character, hope.
Romans 5:3-4

So do not throw away your confidence;
it will be richly rewarded.
You need to persevere so that when you have done
the will of God,
you will receive what He has promised.
Hebrews 10:35-36

The Obstacle

I love volunteering in the classrooms at my children's school. It gives me an opportunity to observe how my child interacts with the other students as well as a chance to develop a relationship with their teachers. Often I am the one who learns something new while I am there. This past week was no exception as God used a toddler to speak to me.

There were several other mothers in Trevor's classroom this week helping with a fall craft rotation. One of the Moms brought her two year old daughter with her and she was enjoying the sights and sounds of first grade. During a break between rotations, as we were sitting in the back of the classroom, the little one was wandering around. She developed a path around and through the maze of tables and she was very intent on her trek. However, as she came around the last table, she encountered an obstacle in her way. A small wipe-off board was propped up in the middle of the floor and the little girl found herself behind it. She was so focused on her goal of moving forward that she did not consider going around it. A small step to the right or the left would have solved her dilemma, but all she could see was that something was in her way! She threw her little arms in the air and squealed for her Mom to rescue her. Her mother rushed over and lifted her over the board and she was happily on her way.

We laughed at her tunnel vision and simplicity of purpose, but suddenly I realized how often I am just like that little girl! Many times I have been that focused on a goal or ambition. With my eyes on the prize I have failed to really notice my environment. How surprised I am when suddenly an obstacle appears and I am blocked from moving forward. If I were to take my eyes off of my personal goal for a moment I might be able to see that there is an easy solution, but usually I just throw my hands up in the air and cry for my Heavenly Father to rescue me!

Many times God will place an obstacle in our path for that very reason. We are to keep our eyes on Him and His purpose, not just *OUR* goals. When He allows something to block us, often He is getting our attention so that we will return our focus to Him. He may not choose to "rescue" us or even to remove the obstacle; instead, He may be calling us to take a look around. We may need the time to discover a solution or time to reevaluate our goals; we may even need to choose an entirely new path. The Bible says that we should not try to squirm out of these situations. Instead, we are to learn from each obstacle and persevere through them so that they can grow us to our full potential.

Dear brothers, is your life full of difficulties and temptations? Then be happy, for when the way is rough, your patience has a chance to grow. So let it grow, and don't try to squirm out of your problems. For when your patience is finally in full bloom, then you will be ready for anything, strong in character, full and complete.
James 1:2-4 (The Living Bible)

You, then, why do you judge your brother?
Or why do you look down on your brother?
For we will all stand before God's judgment seat.
Romans 14:10

You judge by human standards,
I pass judgment on no one.
But if I do judge, my decisions are right,
because I am not alone,
I stand with the Father who sent me.
John 8:15-16

The Master Gardener

The other day, as I was weeding my garden, I noticed how many of the weeds and the plants I grow look similar. Though weeding may not be my favorite task, I do prefer to do it without help from others. I don't think I would appreciate it if someone else decided to surprise me by weeding my garden, even thought the intent would be good. Someone who did not know my plants may think that a plant without a flower was a weed. They may inadvertently pull one of the plants that I treasure. It is not that they would intentionally destroy something that I love; they simply may not recognize the value of the green foliage among the flowering plants. Also, what some consider a weed, others consider a wildflower. It is not within us to always be able to discern the value of a plant in the garden of another.

Many times, I think we set out with good intentions to weed the gardens of our friends and family. Without the intimate knowledge of the Master Gardener, we often can not discern weeds from the valuable plants in their lives. In John 15:1-2, Jesus says, *"I am the true vine and my Father is the gardener. He cuts off every branch in me that bears no fruit. While every branch that does bear fruit He prunes so that it will be even more fruitful."* Only God can come along side of us to weed our gardens, it is not a task for someone else, no matter how good their intentions.

If something in another's life does not produce immediate fruit or a showy bloom, we may decide that it should be discarded, when in truth it has yet to mature and serves instead as beautiful foliage. The parable of the weeds in Matthew talks about this concept. Jesus tells about the enemy sowing weeds among the wheat, and the servants come to the master to ask his directions. *The servants asked him, "Do you want us to go and pull them (the weeds) up?" "No," he answered, "Because while you are pulling the weeds you may root up the wheat with them. Let both grow until the harvest."* (Matthew 13:28b-30a) You see, as servants, we do not have the knowledge to know the difference between the weed and the plant, or the knowledge of how to do the weeding without causing damage to the rest of the garden.

How can we who have not spent the time to cultivate, prepare, plant, and tend the garden, truly know the difference? Instead, we must learn to simply appreciate the gardens of others, allowing the Master Gardener to do the weeding and pruning.

There is only one Lawgiver and Judge (Master Gardener) *the one who is able to save and destroy. But you – who are you to judge* (weed the garden of) *your neighbor?*
James 4:12 (parenthesis – my words)

Let us fix our eyes on Jesus,
the author and perfecter of our faith.
Hebrews 12:2a

Let your eyes look straight ahead,
fix your gaze directly before you.
Make level paths for your feet
and take only ways that are firm.
Do not swerve to the right or the left;
keep your foot from evil.
Proverbs 4:25-27

Focus

We recently returned from a trip to the beach with our family. We stayed in a cottage on a military reservation that was gated and secure and, since we were only a short distance from the beach, we allowed the children to ride their bikes there each day. Before we left, they jumped on to get a head start, hoping to beat our vehicle as we drove with all of the beach stuff. Though they were pedaling as fast as their little legs would carry them, we usually caught up with them about halfway to the parking area. Each time, the kids would glance over their shoulders to see how close we were, and when they did, their bikes began to swerve into our lane. "Look where you are going!" we yelled, but the bikes always turned in the direction of the children's focus.

Our lives will also turn in the direction of our focus. We will move in the direction that we choose to look. If our focus is on worldly things, our lives will become more worldly. On the other hand, if our focus is on the Kingdom of God, our lives will become more godly.

If we are angry about something, and we spend our time focusing on that anger, our hearts will be filled with bitterness and resentment. However, if we choose to let our anger go and we focus instead on forgiveness, our hearts will be filled with peace and joy.

This concept can include our physical focus as well. We choose the things we allow our eyes to see. If we constantly view evil or distorted things, then our hearts will become evil and distorted. Our society is full of those things, and while we may not be able to avoid them all, we do have the power to limit them. TV, movies, internet, magazines, books, and on it goes, visual images bombard our minds everywhere we go. But while the world tries to immerse us in evil, God has provided good.

My camera has an automatic focus; however it can be switched to manual focus. We are much like that as well. Though we tend to automatically focus on the things before us, we can choose! We can turn our thoughts, our emotions, our words, and yes, our physical eyes to more godly things.

Take the time this week to turn your focus to the things of God. Take in the visual images that He has given us; spend time in nature, view a sunset, and read His Word. Use your time in more godly ways; talk with a friend, watch your children play, meditate and pray. Let the good things in life monopolize your thoughts and your focus. You will be amazed at the peace and hope that will take over in your heart.

Choosing our focus is as easy as turning our heads, turning our hearts, and turning to God! Choose today where your focus will be and then your life will follow!

He must turn from evil and do good; he must seek peace and pursue it.
1 Peter 3:11

You too, be patient and stand firm,
because the Lord's coming is near.
James 5:8

Whether you turn to the right or to the left,
your ears will hear a voice behind you, saying,
"This is the way; walk in it."
Isaiah 30:21

Patience and Persistence

I once heard a speaker say that patience was being in the midst of a storm and sitting still, but persistence was pushing through the storm. The hard part is knowing when to sit still and when to push through. There are some storms that call for patience and some that call for persistence, but many storms call for both. We must learn to listen carefully for the spirit to help us discern.

If patience is called for and instead we persist, we may be "pushing ahead" of God. However, if we are to persist and instead we sit still, we are not walking in obedience. God, who is above the storm, will give us constant direction. (See Isaiah 30:21) We must only listen and obey.

Recently I received a literal example of this concept from my Dad. As he was driving home from golfing one afternoon, he was met by a thunderstorm. The storm continued to worsen and soon became severe. The rain and wind and hail became so heavy that he could no longer see and he was forced to stop and wait. He persisted until his vision was blocked, then it was time to be patient. While he was waiting, suddenly it became extremely dark. The wind howled and sticks and debris whirled around the car. Dad hit the gas, and pushed through the wall of the storm. If he had tried to continue driving when he couldn't see, he could have wrecked the car, but if he had remained still when it was time to move, he may have been swept away by the storm.

In the midst of the storms of life, we must focus on God's direction. If we are called to be patient, we must sit still and listen – quiet, but ready to move. If we are called to persist, we must push through - steady and strong, but ready to pause at any moment. We must always trust that God, who is above the storm, is also in the storm with us, protecting and shielding us from the howling wind and whirling debris.

He who dwells in the shelter of the Most High,
will rest in the shadow of the Almighty.
I will say of the Lord,
"He is my refuge and my fortress,
my God, in whom I trust."
Psalm 91:1-2

A man's steps are directed by the Lord.
How then can anyone understand his own way?
Proverbs 20:24

I am the Lord your God,
who teaches you what is best for you,
who directs you in the way you should go.
Isaiah 48:17

Recalculating

When Jerry had to work in Connecticut, I rode along to keep him company. We left Virginia and traveled up the highway with the GPS as our guide. It told us how long our trip would be and which route was best to take. As we neared New York though, the GPS instructed us to go right through the middle of Manhattan. Jerry decided that he did not want to travel through the city, so he took a different route in an effort to go around. Though the territory was unfamiliar, he turned onto the road that seemed best. Immediately, the GPS said "Recalculating," and instructed us to turn off of that road. For many miles, as we continued along our own path, the GPS consistently directed us to get back on the original road. It gave us many chances to redirect, but we kept going on our own path. Finally, after an hour of travel, we supposed that the GPS had conformed to our choice of direction and turned the way that it suggested. Much to our dismay, the road led us right back onto the original path and straight through the city. If we had followed the instructions, we would have made it to the other side of New York City in about 10 minutes, however, following our own path had taken much longer!

God has a plan for our life. By using His Word, prayer, and godly advice, we can be certain that we are headed in the direction He has for us. Often, though, we have a different idea about the way we should go. As we set out on our own path, God gives us many chances to redirect and get back on the right track. We hear His voice in our hearts telling us, "This is not the right way!" Many times we do not listen and we continue to follow our chosen path instead of His.

God allows us that free will in our lives. He will not pick us up and place us on the road that He wants us to take. However, He does know where we are headed and He knows the outcome. If we continue to follow our own way, He will use people, circumstances, and experiences to get us back to that original road. God will see that His purposes are fulfilled!

If we go God's way, though it may not be the way we think is best, we will find the journey to be fulfilling and marked with peace. That is not to say that there will not be bumps in the road, but we will be able to complete that leg of the journey more quickly and be on our way to the next thing.

Our GPS originally told us that we would reach our destination at 10:30pm. With the little side trip of our choosing, we still reached our destination, though it was 11:30pm instead! Following God's way is best. When we get off track, listening to the recalculation is good. Coming back around to God's way after following the wrong path is refreshing. Which of these do you need to do today?

In his heart a man plans his course, but the Lord determines his steps.
Proverbs 16:9

And over all these virtues put on love,
which binds them all together in perfect unity.
Colossians 3:14

Bear with each other and forgive whatever
grievances you may have against one another.
Forgive as the Lord forgave you.
Colossians 3:13

The Fabric of Our Lives

My son, Trevor, once fell and ripped a small hole in the knee of his jeans. Since they were his "old" jeans, we didn't patch the hole and he continued to play in them. Eventually, however, the threads around the tear began to fray and the hole became bigger and bigger. Once a tear has occurred, the fabric around the tear is weaker and more susceptible to further damage.

God knows that when there is pain in a relationship it causes a tear. It may be a small tear if it is a small offense, but often it is so much more. The tearing apart of a relationship causes raw edges, loose threads, an unraveling in our hearts. We must choose whether or not we will let the rawness stay, or be mended with forgiveness. Without forgiveness there is the potential for bitterness, anger, and resentment. These things cause those threads to unravel more and more until it affects the very fabric of our lives. When we choose to forgive, God stitches us back together, mending those edges and healing us so that we don't fall apart. By the way, the crazy thing about bitterness, anger, and resentment is that, when we choose not to forgive, it is *our* threads that unravel, not those of the offender.

If we are to move forward, we must choose forgiveness. We cannot continue to place the next foot in front of the other if our hearts are unraveling. The very functioning of our lives depends on the health of our hearts. Every relationship we have will be affected by this choice. Though we would like a magic formula that would instantly repair the damage that has been done, God does not work that way. Instead, He chooses to mend us one stitch at a time, seam by seam. This way, we make the right choices along the way and ensure that the mending is complete, through and through. You see, the healing depends on us. As we choose to forgive others and ourselves, we allow our focus to shift from our pain to God's grace, and His love seals the loose threads and the unraveling seams.

Examine your hearts today. Are you frayed around the edges? Are you nursing a wound that is becoming worse every day? Are you unraveling at the seams? Start doing the work of forgiveness and allow God to stitch you back together.

For I am poor and needy, and my heart is wounded within me.
Psalm 109:22

Today, if you hear His voice,
do not harden your hearts
as you did in the rebellion.
Hebrews 3:15

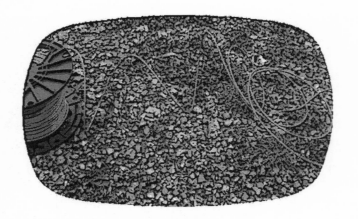

And the peace of God,
which transcends all understanding,
will guard your hearts
and your minds in Christ Jesus.
Philippians 4:7

The Wellspring of Life

Our dog, Ranger, loves our new yard. It is a big, flat, open yard with lots of room to run and play, and plenty of sticks to chew on. The problem is that he also loves the field across the busy road in front of our house. The best solution for us was to install an "invisible fence." This fence consists of a wire connected to a box in the house, and a collar for Ranger that receives a signal from the wire. If Ranger crosses the wire to go outside his safe boundary he will get a shock from the collar to remind him to stay inside the loop.

The wire is a very necessary part of the process. It carries the signal from the box all the way around the yard. If there is even one tiny break in that wire the signal is stopped and the whole system ceases to function. In order to protect the wire, it must be buried a few inches underground. It must be close enough to the surface to send out the signal, but far enough down that it is protected. The dirt from the yard serves as a good cover for the wire; however there is a different problem when the wire crosses the driveway. The rocks in the driveway are pointed and sharp and they may be pushed down into the wire as cars drive across. Those sharp rocks could cut or even sever the wire, causing the system to shut down.

We needed to find something to encase the wire before burying it in the driveway. A hard, rigid, hollow rod seemed to be the obvious choice, but we soon realized that it would be difficult to maneuver the rod in the direction we wanted it to go. We discovered that a piece of garden hose was a better solution. The hose was thick enough to protect the wire from the jagged rocks but flexible enough to be manipulated in direction.

Our hearts are so much like that wire for the invisible fence. They function in a similar way, carrying a signal that protects and guides us through life. Our hearts, like the wire, are also easily injured, and when cut can shut down our entire systems. Often in our attempt to guard our hearts from sharp words and dangerous situations, we encase it in a hard, rigid shell. We will find, though, that a hard heart will not allow us to move in directions that the Holy Spirit leads us. We must learn to guard our hearts, but not let them get hard. When we spend time with God, asking Him for guidance and wisdom in difficult situations, He can provide for us a softer, more flexible protection for our vulnerable hearts. If we allow Him to be our shield, we can continue to love those that hurt us and therefore share His love with them.

There will always be driveways with jagged rocks that we will need to cross, but God offers His love as a covering for us that will protect us from being severed from our source of power.

Above all else, guard your heart, for it is the wellspring of life.
Proverbs 4:23

The light shines in the darkness,
but the darkness has not understood it.
John 1:5

For God, who said,
"Let light shine out of darkness,"
made His light shine in our hearts
to give us the light
of the knowledge of the glory of God
in the face of Christ.
2 Corinthians 4:6

Shining Through

When I am seeking clarity on issues in my life, God often draws me outside at night to talk with him. There is something about a wide open, deep, black sky with millions of tiny stars that reminds me of the amazing power and wonder of my God! I felt drawn there again last night; however, I was disappointed when I discovered that I couldn't see many of the stars. There was a full bright moon but clouds were drifting across the sky. In the distance I could see that the clouds were beginning to thicken. It was fairly warm out though, so I decided to sit and watch the clouds for a while.

Often when I am searching for clarity it seems that instead I find clouds. God seems silent, distant at times. When I am reaching for depth, I find a ceiling. When I began to look into the future, the clouds go on forever and they appear thicker and thicker. Where is the wisdom I am promised in the book of James? Where is God?

As I watched the pattern of clouds moving through the sky last night, something surprised me. The clouds seemed to be opaque as they floated by, but once they passed over the bright, full moon I could see right through them. The light of the moon was shining clearly through each of the clouds. As I watched in amazement I noticed something even more wonderful. The moonlight illuminated the water droplets in the clouds forming a circular rainbow around itself! What a spectacular sight, a rainbow in the dark night sky!

A rainbow is a sign of promise. We are excited to see that sign in the daytime, after a rain, when the sun begins to shine, but how many of us expect to see one at night! I was reminded that though I may be experiencing a time of darkness, though it may feel that clouds are blocking my vision, God's pure and holy light will shine through and His promise remains!

Its truth is seen in Him and you,
because the darkness is passing
and the true light is already shining.
1 John 2:8b

Many are the plans in a man's heart,
but it is the Lord's purpose that prevails.
Proverbs 19:21

I will instruct you and teach you
in the way you should go;
I will counsel you and watch over you.
Psalm 32:8

The Bridge

As I was driving through the Village of Palmyra one day, I began thinking about the new construction that was going on. Apparently, the old bridge that crossed the Rivanna River had become weak and a new bridge was being built. Off in the distance, away from the main road, the work had begun on the new bridge. It was hard to imagine that the road could even connect to that bridge; it seemed so far off the path. I had always used the bridge that I was driving on now and thinking about a change was difficult. Even though I knew in my head that a new bridge would be better, I was comfortable on my same old bridge.

After many months of construction, the new bridge was complete. The connecting road was made and the path to the old bridge was blocked off. It was uncomfortable to make the turn onto the new road, since I had driven the old path so many times, but after weeks of practice, the new became comfortable.

The old road was destroyed and broken up, grass began to grow in its place, and it was sometimes difficult to imagine that it was even there. There were remnants that gave it away though, and every once in a while, the old memories of driving on that bridge enter my mind. Though the new bridge is in a different place, it still leads me to the same destination. Though the old way had become weak and no longer worked to get me where I needed to go, a new way was made for me so that I am still able to continue on. I am thankful now for that new way.

God has a plan, a direction for our lives. He will make a way for us. If the old way, the way we are used to becomes weak and no longer works, He will make a new way. Often, we don't want to let go of our old ways since they are comfortable. It can be hard to let go of something that has been in our lives for a long time. But God knows when the old is no longer working and He begins in advance to prepare the new way for us. Once the connecting road has been made, it is up to us to change our direction.

There will always be memories of the old way, even after the grass has begun to grow, but we should be thankful for the one who loves us and creates a way that gets us to our destination. We must determine which is more important, the path we travel or the destination. Let the Lord lead you in the new paths of your life. Don't cling to the old, but embrace the new. He will bring you back to the plan, the direction He has for your life.

For He guards the course of the just and protects the way of His faithful ones.
Then you will understand what is right and just and fair – every good path.
Proverbs 2:8-9

"But encourage one another daily,
as long as it is called Today,
so that none of you may be
hardened by sin's deceitfulness."
Hebrews 3:13

"He comes alongside us when we go
through hard times, and before you know it,
He brings us alongside someone else who is going
through hard times so that we can be there
for that person just as God was there for us."
2 Corinthians 1: 4 (The Message)

Filling in the Cracks

Last spring, Jerry and I decided to lay a sidewalk in his front yard. The area was anything but level and we were using stones that fit together like a puzzle. We had planned to use sand as our base so we dumped piles of it along the path of the future walkway. After spreading the sand and leveling it out, we laid our stones one by one. Though the stones were created to fit together, there were still cracks between them. Once we had completed the path, we scooped more sand on top and swept it over the stones to fill in the cracks and to keep them from shifting out of place. The stones created the beauty of the sidewalk, but the thousands of grains of sand made the walkway stable and complete.

God desires for us to be like that sand in the lives of those around us. We can not be all things to all people, but we are to be one thing to all people. We are to be encouragers. With our encouragement, we help to level the lives of those on uneven ground as well as fill in the gaps where their lives do not quite fit together. I am aware that not all women are mothers; however, God has given us, as women, the nature to nurture and encourage others. We have unlimited opportunity to fill in the cracks in the lives of other women.

I recently wrote a list of the needs of women that I had come across in my community. Within moments, I was able to fill two sheets of paper with needs that ranged from emotional to spiritual to physical. Most of those needs could easily be addressed through other women who had already faced similar circumstances. When a woman finds herself on uneven ground, a place that is out of her comfort zone and unfamiliar, the mentorship and encouragement of a woman who has been there is invaluable. Women can literally use their experiences and wisdom from God as a foundation to level the way for another.

Most women on a firm foundation still find that there are places in their lives that do not fit together. They may have small cracks that need to be filled in healthy and Godly ways. As women, we can help to fill those gaps with small acts of encouragement and friendship: a smile, a hug, a note, or phone call, a warm meal, or a cool drink on a hot day, fresh cut flowers, a shoulder to cry on, a listening ear, a word of wisdom, or a gentle reminder, a book to read, a place to rest, a touching tune, an act of kindness, or an act of service. These are the grains of sand that hold it all together. With the encouragement of another, we find the courage to continue.

Whether we are called to help level an uneven path, to stand in the gap, or simply to help fill the cracks in someone's life, we are called to be encouragers. Take a look around, see the needs, and pray for direction and discernment. God will use you to bless another as He will use another to bless you!

Let's see how inventive we can be in encouraging love and helping out,
not avoiding worshipping together as some do but spurring each other on,
especially as we see the big Day approaching.
Hebrews 10:25 (The Message)

Be beautiful inside, in your hearts,
with the lasting charm of a gentle and quiet spirit
which is so precious to God.
1 Peter 3:4 (Living Bible)

Finally brothers, whatever is true,
whatever is noble,
whatever is right, whatever is admirable
if anything is excellent or praiseworthy
– think about such things.
Philippians 4:8

Under My Skin

My stepdaughter, Renee, recently visited the allergist. She was breaking out in hives every night and we couldn't figure out why. The allergist gave her a skin test in which he exposed her to several items - and she tested positive to all of them! Milk, trees, dust mites, the family dogs, you name it and she is allergic to it. The doctor reassured Renee that she wouldn't have to stop drinking milk or petting Rover. You see, she only reacts to them if they get under her skin! When Renee's skin is dry, like most skin in the winter months, she itches. When she itches, she scratches. When Renee scratches, the allergens get "under her skin" and her skin reacts - badly! What was the doctor's solution? We need to keep Renee's skin soft. Using moisturizing soap and lotion on her skin keeps it from getting dry and itchy. When she is comfortable in her skin, no allergens get in!

This made me start thinking about the things that get under my skin! As far as I know, I am not allergic to anything, but plenty of things do make me react badly! I have noticed that when children do not behave in public (including my own), they get under my skin. They may not cause me to break out in a physical rash, but the reaction that I sometimes have is just as ugly. Bad customer service or someone that treats me rudely is another thing that tends to irritate me. There are many things that I could add to this list, just like the list of the items that causes Renee's reaction. The thing is, I can do something about it. I do not need to avoid these things, or seek to cut them from my life; instead I need to work on preventing my reaction.

When I focus on the negative things, such my problems or the problems of others, it causes my spirit to become dry and thirsty. When all of my attention is used on worldly issues like money and success, my spirit becomes dehydrated. When my energies are spent because I am so busy doing things, my spirit becomes parched. When my spirit is dry, I am uncomfortable. When I am uncomfortable, I am easily irritated! What is the solution? I must keep my spirit soft!

When I focus on positive things, such as my blessings, my spirit becomes refreshed. When my attention is given to godly things, I am given Living water to drink. When my energies are renewed because of time I have spent with the Lord, then my spirit is also renewed. When my spirit is revived, I am more than comfortable; I am full of love, joy, peace, patience, kindness, goodness, faithfulness, gentleness, and self-control. When I am full of the Spirit, nothing can get under my skin! It's not that the irritating things aren't around me, but I can instead appreciate the person instead of their actions. I can respond with compassion and understanding instead of ugliness.

The Bible states that I am responsible for my words and my actions. I must do what I can to keep my spirit soft and my countenance sweet. Living water is readily available; it is up to me to take the drink!

My people have committed two sins: They have forsaken me, the spring of living water, and have dug their own cisterns, broken cisterns that cannot hold water.
Jeremiah 2:13

In repentance and rest is your salvation,
in quietness and trust is your strength.
Isaiah 30:15

Trust God from the bottom of your heart;
don't try to figure out everything on your own.
Listen for God's voice in everything you do,
everywhere you go; He's the one who will
keep you on track.

The Climb

At one time, I was a leader in a high-adventure explorer post (an upper level of Boy Scouts). We had taken the group rock climbing to Seneca Rocks in West Virginia. I had never been climbing but I was really looking forward to a new adventure. After a very strenuous hike, we reached the rock face we would be climbing. I spent a good while watching the boys climb. Some were natural climbers and some struggled, but they all made it up and rappelled back down. From the bottom, it was easy to call out footholds and hand-holds and help the climber find a strategy to work his way up.

After watching for the better part of the morning, I was ready to try. I got hooked into the Swiss seat, clipped on the carabineer, had the ropes checked, called out the commands, and began my ascent. One of the other leaders was on belet (holding my rope) and assured me that I would not fall. I climbed for what seemed like an eternity until I got stuck. I couldn't seem to find a place to move my foot that felt secure. The leader was below and just like when I had been in his position, he could clearly see the right path for me. He was calling out directions, but I didn't trust him – it just didn't feel possible that I could reach and not fall. "Remember," he shouted up to me, "I have you – you won't fall!" How many times have the Lord and I been in the same spot? He is in the position to call out the directions – He can see the path – He tells me which foot and which hand to move. He is holding me firmly so even if I miss or let go, I won't fall! But do I trust Him?

The leader on belet had confidence that I could make it to the top and he wanted to see me succeed, so he told me that he wouldn't let me down until I completed the climb. At first, I was irritated with that announcement because I was tired and frustrated, and I just wanted to quit. But since he had the rope (and because I didn't want to disappoint him), I accepted the challenge and climbed on. With the help of that leader, I was able to move beyond the place where I was stuck and reached a higher spot. But wouldn't you know – I got stuck again – and this time I looked down! Frustration gave way to fear, and fear gave way to exhaustion. I felt defeated and completely unable to hang on. As my fingers slipped from the rock and I swung away from the wall, an amazing thing happened – I didn't fall! That leader had the rope, the rope had me, and I discovered that it was okay to rest. Now that I could trust the rope and the leader, I was free to follow his commands and take those "faith stretches" because I knew I was secure.

I can think of many times when I am working so hard at my life: striving to be obedient, following my calling, trying to do the right thing. But I get frustrated, fearful, and exhausted. Sometimes what I need to do is to stop climbing, let go, and rest in Him. He has us securely – we will not fall when we trust Him. When we are ready, we can resume the climb. When we have "let go" and rested in Him we will find that we are secure and it is safe to reach beyond what we think we can do.

After resting, it was a short climb to the top. What a great feeling to accomplish that purpose even though I had been ready to give up twice. What a blessing to have someone who believed in me, pushed me to a new level of success, supported me and had been merciful to me. What a blessing to have someone who could lead me along the clear path and help me safely reach a new height. Our lives consist of one new face after another. God chooses our challenges according to what He knows we can and should achieve. We must rely on Him for clear direction, mercy, support, and encouragement when we think it is impossible. Remember, our Lord is always on belet!

God, listen to me shout, bend an ear to my prayer, when I'm far from anywhere,
down to my last gasp, I call out, "Guide me up High Rock Mountain!"
Psalm 61:1-2 (The Message)

*I know that nothing good lives in me
that is my sinful nature.
For I have the desire to do what is good,
but I cannot carry it out.
Romans 7:18*

*In the same way, the Spirit helps us in our weakness.
We do not know what we ought to pray for,
but the Spirit Himself intercedes for us with groans
that words cannot express.
Romans 8:26*

The Big, Ugly Tree

There is a big, ugly tree in our front yard. The first thing Jerry said about the house when we decided to buy it was, "I can't wait to cut down that tree!" We have been here almost a year and it still stands. The tree is some sort of an evergreen. Its branches and needles are droopy and it looks kind of sad. Maybe the tree is sad because of the side that has been lopped off to make way for an electrical line. There is poison ivy underneath the tree and every time the kids go underneath of it for a ball or another lost toy, they come out itchy. The worst part is that the tree is so big that it blocks the view of the house. Anyone driving down the road sees the huge, neglected tree, not our lovely home. Now, I know you are wondering why it has taken us so long to cut down that tree. Truthfully, we are just too busy doing other things. We don't like the tree, but it doesn't seem to be hurting anything and there are so many other projects to do. We know that cutting it down won't be easy because of the position with the house and the power line, so we put it off until later. And the big ugly tree still stands.

I have some things in my life that are a lot like that tree. Some ugly things, things that have stood too long, things that have been neglected. Most of those things aren't really hurting anyone unless they get underneath of them where the poison lies. But they are out front, large and lopsided, for everyone to see. The worst part is that anyone going by tends to see those things and not the part of me that is lovely. These are things that I want to get rid of – have wanted to for a very long time, but there are so many other projects to work on. I know that to cut these things out of my life will take a lot of work. There will be many obstacles to maneuver around and it will take time, so I have put them off until later. And the big, ugly tree still stands.

I suppose we could call a tree service to come and take down the tree for us. They could probably chop it down in one day, grind the stump, clean up the mess, and it would be done. But tree services cost a lot of money and we are capable of cutting down the tree ourselves. Jerry has cut down other large trees in the yard, so I know we can do it. We have a neighbor that has a tree service and he offered to come and help. He has the expertise to help us maneuver around the difficult places and it won't cost us as much, but we would have the confidence that nothing would get damaged. All we have to do is make the decision to do it – and ask him. And the big, ugly tree still stands.

I have a God who is able to help me too. He won't come and remove the things for me, for that would cost too much. When something like that is done for us, we don't learn how to keep the big, ugly things out of our lives. Instead, God has offered to help me maneuver around the difficult places. You see, He has the expertise, the know-how, and He loves to help us! All I have to do is to make the decision – and ask Him. I think its time to take down the big, ugly tree!

Do not be dismayed. I am your God. I will strengthen you;
I will help you; I will uphold you with my victorious right hand.
Isaiah 41:10

58

Share with God's people who are in need.
Practice hospitality.
Romans 12:13

"Give, and it will be given to you.
A good measure, pressed down,
shaken together and running over,
will be poured into your lap.
For with the measure you use,
it will be measured to you."
Luke 6:38

Overflowing With Blessings

The call came while I was at the soccer field waiting for the kids to finish practice. My husband was frantic! A stopped-up plumbing fixture had unknowingly overflowed and was left to run until it was discovered over an hour later. The bathroom floor was full of water, so Jerry headed to the basement to grab the shop vac. There he found that the water had come through the ceiling and filled up two thousand square feet about a quarter of an inch deep. While he stood downstairs with water showering all around him, the power flickered and went out. What were we to do? We called our friends!

Within a short period of time, seven of our friends and family showed up with shop vacs, generators, and great attitudes of encouragement and help! Praise God, the power outage was an area problem and was not caused by the water leak, as we had originally thought. The power soon returned and we made quick work of sucking up the pool in the basement. We carried wet rugs, toys, and clothes out of the kids' rooms and tore down ceilings that were sagging with water. My mom packed the children's things and they went to a friend's house for a clean, dry place to sleep. One of our friends even commented on our recent renovation that she was able to appreciate through all of the mess! What an amazing night!

We were flooded by encouragement, showered by friendship, and overflowing with thankfulness for all of the blessings we have in our life! Even in the midst of disaster, God showed us a clear picture of what fellowship is supposed to be. No one complained that their plans for the evening were interrupted; everyone came and gave of their time generously. We were blessed, our home was restored, and the damage was minimal. This is friendship, this is love!

God calls us to have intimate relationships with other believers. He even commands for us to love one another, to encourage one another, and to give to one another. I hope that we would respond to others in time of need in the same way that our friends and family have responded to us.

Here are a few tips that I learned from our support that night.

~ Respond quickly in time of need
~Come with the necessities – great attitudes and equipment if needed
~See through the mess and recognize the good – then point it out
~Laugh a lot
~Enjoy the opportunity to fellowship regardless of the circumstances
~Roll up your pant legs, get your feet wet, don't mind the bumps and bruises
~Praise God together, it could have been worse!

Two are better than one, because they have a good return for their work:
If one falls down, his friend can help him up.
But pity the man who falls and has no one to help him up!
Ecclesiastes 4:9-10

We ought always to thank God for you,
brothers, and rightly so,
because your faith is growing more and more
and the love every one of you
has for each other is increasing.
2 Thessalonians 1:3

And even we Christians, although we have the Holy
Spirit within us as a foretaste of future glory,
also groan to be released from pain and suffering.
We, too, wait anxiously for that day when God will
give us our full rights as his children, including the
new bodies he has promised us – bodies that will
never be sick again and will never die.
Romans 8:23(Living Bible)

Growing Pains

I love spring! The green poking through the ground where my plants and bulbs are beginning to wake from the winter gets me so excited. The tiny blooms on my lilac bush almost sent me right over the edge this morning. But I have to wonder if the bud of new leaves, coming through the bark on the branches of the trees, feels a little like cutting teeth? New growth is not usually comfortable.

When my son, Carter, was small, he would sometimes scream and cry about pain in his legs. It really scared us, but after a while (and a few doctor's visits) we figured out that he was experiencing growing pains. My normally picky eater would suddenly gobble down everything in sight for several days. The eating binge would be followed by a series of days of crying about the pains in his legs. Then suddenly, one day, Carter would wake up and his pants would be an inch too short! He was a child that grew in spurts.

I have noticed that my spiritual growth works in much the same way. I wish that I was the kind of person that just steadily grew in my faith but, for me, that would be too easy. Instead, I tend to be one that grows in spurts. I will suddenly devour the Word like I can't get enough. I will read and study, or maybe be involved in an intense Bible study group where I am learning something new. Sometimes it might be a topic that I have been struggling with, or sometimes it is something that I thought I had already conquered. At any rate, God begins to fill me with His nutrition and then, of course, I must grow.

This period of time where I am filled with His truth generally transitions into a time of growing pains. As I said before, new growth is not comfortable. In order to grow, something must move, stretch, or even be torn apart. The new thoughts and feelings displace the old ones, and something in me must die to make way for the new growth. Ouch!

Just like Carter, though, when I have made it through my time of groaning and pain, suddenly I awake one day to find that I have grown. The new ideas and feelings that I struggled with now fit comfortably. My character and my spirit have grown an inch or so. The new growth has burst through and the old is gone. The broken places have healed and the scars are beginning to disappear. The beauty of the blooms and new leaves take over the pain of the pushing through and spring has come!

If you are experiencing growing pains, take heart! They will pass. Soon, the beauty of the new growth will overshadow the pain. Whether your faith is stretching or your mind is changing, it will not last forever. Don't be afraid to grow, just trust God and hang in there, spring is almost here!

After you have suffered a little while, our God, who is full of kindness through Christ, will give you His eternal glory. He personally will come and pick you up, and set you firmly in place, and make you stronger than ever.
1Peter 5:10

But the fruit of the Spirit is love, joy, peace,
patience, kindness, goodness, faithfulness,
gentleness, and self-control.
Galatians 5:22

If I have the gift of prophecy and fathom all
mysteries and all knowledge,
and if I have a faith that can move mountains,
but have not love, I am nothing.
1 Corinthians 13:2

Bitter Fruit

We planted our first garden this year. We were very excited about growing our own food and it was really fun deciding what fruits and vegetables to plant. Amazingly, we did get some good things out of it, especially at the beginning of the season. Our green beans and peas did fairly well and we had quite a few tomatoes. However, near the end of the summer, we experienced somewhat of a drought and though we watered frequently, it was not enough for the cantaloupe and watermelons to survive.

There were a few small melons in the garden and even though they were not fully mature, we decided to give them a try. The color on the outside was good and even the inside of the cantaloupe seemed ripe, but when we tasted it the fruit was bitter! The watermelon also appeared ripe on the outside, but inside, the flesh had no color or taste. Though the fruit was still attached to the branch, the branch had withered and was no longer attached to the vine.

Just as our melons needed their life source in order to provide nutrients for growth, our spirits also need nutrition. The fruit that we bear is evidence of the life that we have. If our lives are void of God's truth and love, we will not produce good fruit. In fact, we may produce fruit that is beautiful on the outside but bitter or tasteless inside.

We may do many good things in our lives. We may donate to charities, volunteer for good causes, and attempt to be good people. However, without the love of Christ in our hearts, all of these things are meaningless. They are empty and hollow, devoid of the richness and taste of God's truth. When our branches are no longer connected to the vine, we cannot ripen or grow.

How can we be assured that we are connected to the vine? What can we do to avoid withering in the drought that will surely come during seasons in our lives? The one sure way is to remain in the presence of God – reading His Word, talking with Him, listening to His voice, fellowshipping with His people!

Some parts of our lives are easy to grow, others require effort. Our spirits must remain connected to the sustainer of life in order to grow. Check your fruit! Is it bitter or without taste, or is it ripening in the Son, full of the rich flavor that comes from being infused with truth and love?

I am the vine; you are the branches. If a man remains in me and I in him,
he will bear much fruit; apart from me you can do nothing.
John 15:5

And this is love:
that we walk in obedience to His commands.
2 John 1:6

My eyes are ever on the Lord,
for only He will release my feet from the snare.
Psalm 25:15

The Walk

Today I took my new puppy and my five year old lab for a walk. I am absolutely exhausted! The puppy tried to climb up my leg, wrestle with Ranger, and got tangled up in the leash many times. But I expected that from the puppy. Since he has not been on many walks with a leash, he has not yet experienced the discipline of my training.

Ranger, on the other hand, has walked with me many times. He knows the commands and signals, and he is familiar with the feel of the leash. Ranger has never been easy to walk though, because he always wants to pull ahead. He wants to lead the walk instead of walking with me. It makes our trips together difficult rather than enjoyable. I wish that he could grasp the concept of letting me lead, instead of forcing me to constantly pull and tug at him.

Today, because of the puppy, I kept Ranger on a very short leash. When he pulled ahead, I tightened the tension; when he stayed by my side, I gave him slack. By the last part of our walk, he seemed to relax and I noticed that I didn't have to pull on him as much. Maybe, if we practice every day, we will soon be able to walk together without a struggle.

I know that I am much like Ranger. I am rarely content to walk quietly by my Master. I have walked with Him for a long time, but I have a tendency to pull ahead and I always want to try my own way. I know that He loves me, and the leash that he has on me is not to restrict my freedom, but for my protection and guidance. I choose to wear it and to walk with Him, yet I still try to lead.

I know that if I would learn to walk quietly by His side, if I would learn to keep my eyes on Him, watching and listening for His commands and signals, then our walk together would be delightful. Both my Master and I would enjoy our journey so much more, if only I would remember that He is my Master.

I'm not afraid when you walk at my side.
Your trusty shepherd's crook makes me feel secure.
Psalm 23 (The Message)

Since we live by the Spirit,
let us keep in step with the Spirit.
Galatians 5:25

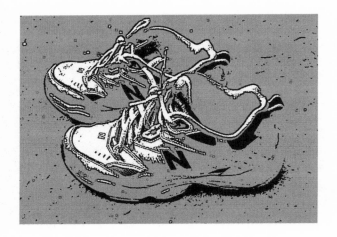

But as for you, continue in what you have learned
and have become convinced of, because you know
those from whom you learned it.
2 Timothy 3:14

Break It Down

When I was an aerobics instructor, I was taught to lead the class in a particular way that made it possible for everyone to follow the routine. First, I would teach a small piece of the routine that would only involve a few steps. After repeating that piece several times, I would teach the participants a new set of steps. When the second set was mastered, we would put the two pieces together. Then, I would teach the final set and add it to the first two. Soon, we could easily go through the entire routine because we had taken the time to break it all down. Each set had been learned and practiced separately, but together they were complete.

I really believe this is what Peter is speaking about in 2 Peter 1:5-8. Peter writes about seven virtues that we should possess in order to have an effective and fruitful Christian life; faith, goodness, knowledge, self-control, perseverance, godliness, brotherly kindness, and love. Paul does not say that these virtues should all be attained at once. He also does not recommend that each should be perfected individually, but rather, that we should add one to another in increasing measure. Likewise, none of these is enough on its own. We need to practice each virtue, and then add it on to the others as we learn them.

As each of these virtues increases, the others should be increasing as well. If our faith becomes stronger, then our goodness shall be more forthcoming. As we display more goodness, our knowledge must increase to support it. When we gain more knowledge, we will need more self-control to exercise what we have learned. As our self-control increases, we will need to persevere more to endure the trials. As we continue to persevere, our godliness will naturally increase. As we become more godly, we must show our kindness to our brothers. And finally as our kindness grows, it will mature into love. Breaking them down makes each virtue more manageable to learn, adding them together makes a complete routine!

For this very reason, make every effort to add to your faith goodness;
and to goodness, knowledge, and to knowledge, self-control;
and to self-control, perseverance; and to perseverance, godliness;
and to godliness, brotherly kindness; and to brotherly kindness, love.
For if you possess these qualities in increasing measure,
they will keep you from being ineffective and unproductive in your
knowledge of our Lord Jesus Christ.
2 Peter 1:5-8

If it is possible, as far as it depends on you,
live at peace with everyone.
Romans 12:18

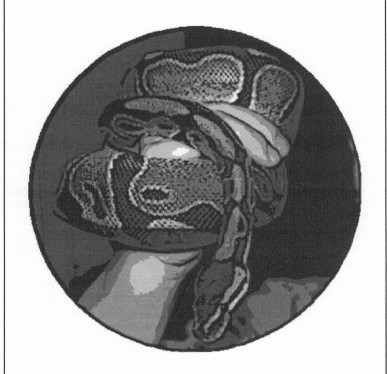

Therefore let us stop passing
judgment on one another.
Instead, make up your mind not
to put any stumbling block
or obstacle in your brother's way.
Romans 14:13

Striking Out

Those of you who know my family may not be surprised to hear that we got a new pet. However, you may be surprised to hear that the new pet is a snake – a ball python to be exact! The children and Jerry love it, and though I refuse to hold it, or feed it, or clean its cage, I am fascinated by its beauty and its ways.

The snake is housed in a very nice cage downstairs in our TV room. It is a docile, rather affectionate creature who sleeps most of the day. This particular snake has been handled often and treated with respect so he is not aggressive or mean and he doesn't bite. Recently, though, we did have the opportunity to learn that there are a couple of things that will get his britches in a bunch!

Our cage is lined across the front with two layers of screen. This screen combined with the light in his cage prevents the snake from being able to see well outside of his own environment. When the dogs come downstairs, they like to sleep under the cage and the smell of them drives the snake crazy! The first time they came down after he arrived, he slithered back and forth across the floor of his cage smelling them, and when there was a sudden movement, he struck the cage. I also like to fold laundry in that room. The other day as I folded, I shook a sheet out right in front of the snake cage. Though he had been sleeping, the noise combined with sudden movement and a flash of color roused him and, again, he struck at the wire!

I have decided that most of us are something like this snake. We are usually well mannered and easy to get along with. We normally enjoy attention and companionship and we respond well to love and respect. There are some things for all of us though, that will get our britches in a bunch! Whenever we are in an environment that is uncomfortable or a place that prevents us from seeing clearly, we are always more easily startled or frightened. Just like our snake, fear or frustration can cause us to strike out. There are two lessons that we can learn here.

First, unlike the snake, we can strive to react slower in situations that are new and different. We can use discernment, forgiveness, and wisdom in life so that we strike out less often. Though we may not be able to see clearly outside of our own environment, we can trust that God can see and will protect and guide us. Second, it does no good for us to be mad at the snake; instead, it makes more sense to investigate what causes him to get upset. Understanding encourages us to be compassionate, and when we know how to prevent a person's fear we can increase his comfort. In an environment of comfort, love, and respect, a relationship can blossom and grow.

How we act, *and* how we react says much about our faith. God calls us to be wise, both in our own circumstances and in the circumstances of others.

Everyone should be quick to listen, slow to speak and slow to become angry,
for man's anger does not bring about the righteous life that God desires.
James 1:19-20

Be still before the Lord
and wait patiently for Him.
Psalm 37:7a

In repentance and rest is your salvation,
in quietness and trust is your strength.
Isaiah 30:15

The Still Place

I walked the creek today. Normally, I am drawn to the places where I can hear the water tumbling over the stones. The sound of the water gurgling, trickling, rushing is a soothing sound to me. I enjoy watching the water find its way around the rocks, forming interesting patterns, carrying with it leaves and twigs. I like to observe what will make its way around the rocks and what will become trapped.

Today, though, I was drawn to a different place. I stopped at an area where the water was quiet, almost still, and for some reason it filled me with wonder. How can the same body of water be rushing before, and rushing after, but in the middle be so quiet and almost not moving? The water seemed to form a pool, an oasis of peace in the midst of busyness. There was no sound. Leaves gently floated instead of tumbling. There were no ripples. It made no sense. Shouldn't the momentum of before push this water along at the same pace? Didn't the motion further downstream have to come from this same water? It seemed to say that it is okay to stop and rest for a while. It is alright for life to virtually halt. Peace is good and natural. The busyness and excitement will return in due time.

I noticed that the place where the water was still and quiet was also deeper and clearer. The areas where the water rushed was often shallow, full of rocks, limbs, and other obstacles. Also, the movement of the water itself made it difficult to see below the surface.

In life, I often prefer and gravitate towards the rushing water. I find the busyness of life – the patterns, the sounds, stimulating and exciting. But I wonder if it is the distraction that I enjoy most. As I have taken a sabbatical from my life lately, a quietness and stillness has naturally formed. It has been a bit frightening. To give up all of the rushing and the momentum, to be quiet and still, is to give up control. I have to trust that I will be given the opportunity to have that movement again. Am I moving now? Yes, I must be, just as that water in the still place was moving. However, it is a peaceful, contemplative moving with depth and clarity that is not possible in rushing water.

Now, when I get to a place of excitement and tumbling, the momentum is no longer mine, but God's. What freedom to know that I can be still, that I don't have to keep moving just to keep that momentum going. I can be free to enjoy the peace now and the rushing, tumbling, excitement when it comes.

He leads me beside quiet waters, He restores my soul.
Psalm 23:2b-3a

72

In the morning, O Lord, you hear my voice;
in the morning I lay my requests before you
and wait in expectation.
Psalm 5:3

If you, then, though you are evil,
know how to give good gifts to your children,
how much more will your Father in heaven
give good gifts to those who ask him!
Matthew 7:11

Little Blessings

I am always amazed at the way God blesses us, but I think it is the little blessings that delight me the most. I am sometimes blown away by how personal God is and how He can be so quick to meet my everyday needs.

This past week has been an unusually busy one. I have had a lot on my plate, including numerous opportunities to encourage other people. By lunchtime yesterday, I was depleted and feeling discouraged. On the way home from an appointment, I poured my heart out to God, expressing my own need for encouragement. As I was driving, I noticed the beautiful yellow wildflowers that crop up along side the road this time of year. "Oh God," I said, "I sure would love to have some of those!" When I arrived home, I was so exhausted that I laid down for a nap. I must have really needed it because I slept for three hours! I woke up to the sound of my husband and children in the kitchen doing homework. As I walked into the room to find out how their day was, I was surprised by a large vase of those beautiful yellow flowers on my kitchen table! Unaware of my morning prayer, Jerry and the kids had stopped on the way home from school to pick them for me.

What an encouragement! Of course, I thanked my family for their thoughtfulness and they were pleased by my joy. However, I must give the credit for the blessing to the Lord. He heard my plea, noticed my despair, and responded immediately.

Often, I think we hesitate to ask God for little things and save up our requests for major events in our lives. Do we think He is too busy or maybe that He doesn't care about our every day? Are we afraid that we may use up our blessings or are we not sure that we should approach the throne with something so silly?

The Bible tells us that in everything we should present our requests to God. It tells us that God loves to give us good things and that He hears us when we pray. He does not set a limit on our requests nor is He too busy or distracted to bother with our small stuff. He loves us and cares about every detail of our lives. While He may not grant every wish that we have, or fix our every problem, He does truly care and will provide for our needs.

We are also told in Scripture that we must have the faith and dependence on God that a child has for his parents. I have children and they are not afraid to ask for anything! I can't always give them the desires of their heart, but when it is available to me *and* it is good for them, I delight in honoring their requests. God is available. He is waiting to hear from you. He wants to spend time with you, He wants to encourage you, and He wants to give you the desires of your heart. Pour out your requests to the Lord, then give Him the praise and thanksgiving for all of the blessings you are about to receive!

Do not be anxious about anything, but in everything, by prayer and petition, with thanksgiving, present your requests to God.
Philippians 4:6

Immediately Jesus reached out
His hand and caught him.
"You of little faith," he said,
"why did you doubt?"
Matthew 14:31

Now may the God of peace,
who brought again from the dead
our Lord Jesus, equip you with all
you need for doing His will.
Hebrews 13:21

Sink or Walk

I feel like I am drowning! Only a few moments ago, I was walking on solid footing, feeling on top of the world. Life was exciting, on the edge, fun. Then, suddenly, the refreshing breeze that was blowing through my hair became a whipping wind around me and the water that was lapping around my ankles became giant waves threatening to engulf me. I forgot the gentle voice that called me out here in the first place, and I began to hear a whisper in my ear telling me that I should be very afraid! What in the world was I thinking? I can't do this- I should have never stepped out like this! And then, I began to sink! Does this sound familiar? Have you ever stepped out of the boat- taken a risk- only to have fear and doubts grip you? Have you ever felt called to something bigger than yourself and then wondered how you ever thought that you could make it? If you have, then you can identify with Peter!

Peter watched Jesus walk on water. Then when Jesus called him, Peter hopped over the side of the boat and out onto the water himself! Can you imagine being so bold? Peter must have felt exhilarated! He had spent a large portion of his life on that sea; after all he was a fisherman. He knew of the dangers and the mysteries of the water. He had leaned over the edge many times to pull his net full of fish into the boat. Certainly he had been in the water at times, since we know from a later account that he was a great swimmer. But this time was different, this time Peter was doing something that he was incapable of doing himself. As Peter walked toward Jesus on top of the water, he must have marveled at the feel of the water under his feet, the smell of the salt air in his face. And then, something happened...

Peter began to change his focus. When he leapt over the side of the boat, he was focusing on Jesus. When Peter's feet touched the water, he was focusing on Jesus. When he began to walk on the water, he was focusing on Jesus. But Peter became distracted. The wind, the water, possibly the voices of disbelief behind him, whatever it was, Peter changed his focus. As soon as he began to focus on the things happening around him, he stopped focusing on Jesus. And as soon as his focus changed, he began to sink! You see, Peter could never actually walk on water. It was Jesus who could walk on water. When Peter allowed Jesus' power to flow through him, then he was able to do what Jesus could do.

I cannot do the things that God has called me to do. Alone, *I* do not have that kind of power. If I allow Christ to work through me, then and only then, are all things possible. I must keep my focus on Him. I must not let the things of the world distract me. I must not take my eyes off of Him for one moment. When I do, I lose that power and I begin to sink.

In this New Year, I am full of goals and aspirations. I am full of the desire to follow God wherever He calls me. I am feeling called to many things that are out of the boat, over the edge, and bigger than me! I pray that I will be able to keep my focus on Jesus, and keep my head (and my heels) above the water!

Jesus looked at them and said,
"With man this is impossible, but with God all things are possible."

How sweet are you words to my taste,
sweeter than honey to my mouth!
Psalm 119:103

Now to Him who is able to do immeasurably more
than all we ask or imagine, according to His power
that is at work within us.
Ephesians 3:20

Banana Pancakes

As a special treat the other day, I made banana pancakes. I didn't tell the kids what kind they were, so immediately they asked, "What kind of pancakes are these?" I decided to let them guess. Right away Carter guessed blueberry. "Carter," I said, "Do you see any blueberries in them?" "Well, no." "Do they smell like blueberry pancakes?" "Not really." "Do you taste the blueberries?" He shook his head. The other kids continued guessing. "Are they peach? Chocolate Chip? Raspberry?" They guessed everything they could think of, but Carter continued to guess blueberry. He just wouldn't take no for an answer.

Have you ever tried to make something what it wasn't? Many times, I have been so sure that something should be a certain way that I have continued to think that it was. When I get a particular answer or idea in my head, it is very difficult for me to change my mind- even when it is obvious to everyone around that I am wrong. It may not smell, look, or taste like what I think it is, but doggone it, I am right!

Eventually I told the children that the pancakes were made with bananas. Of course, then it was obvious to them what that taste was- except for Carter. He was still sure that they were blueberry pancakes! The pancakes were good, they had a sweet taste, they were full of nutrition, and there were plenty to fill their little bellies. But that was not enough for him; he had gotten stuck on the idea of blueberries! It was as if he asked enough times, maybe it would be so.

God gives us such good things. He provides for us and enjoys doing so. The things He gives us are sweet to taste, full of goodness, and plenty to fill our cups. But sometimes we get stuck on another idea. We think we must have it a certain way. Our relationships, our jobs, our homes- we know what we want and we want it now! God wants us to ask for the desires of our hearts, but we must learn to be content with what He gives us. Maybe He will give us banana pancakes instead of blueberry. Maybe He is saving the blueberries until they are fully ripe, or maybe, He just knows that the bananas are better for us at the time. Whatever His reason, we must learn to accept and even enjoy what He gives us.

The kids couldn't figure out the flavor of the pancakes because they were relying on their knowledge and not their sense of taste. We must learn to put our own ideas aside and use our other senses to discover what God has for us. Learn to see what God is doing in and around your life. Learn to smell the aroma of His goodness in the blessings of your day. And finally, learn to taste the richness of what He puts on your plate. Allow His provision to fill your life with the fullness that only He can give!

Taste and see that the Lord is good.
Psalm 34:8

You have set our iniquities before you,
our secret sins in the light of your presence.
Psalm 90:8

Have nothing to do with the fruitless deeds of
darkness, but rather expose them.
Ephesians 5:11

Whitewashed

Recently, we decided to try to spruce up the basement a bit. The children's rooms are down there, as well as our family room area, so we thought that painting the drywall and floor would really brighten it up. However, when we tore down some of the sheetrock to make a repair from a former leak, we discovered a dark secret behind the walls – Mold! Though we had fixed the leak, there was still evidence of a problem. The moisture had built up behind the walls and, left alone, the problem was literally growing!

We were faced with a decision. We could simply clean out the mold that we could see, patch up the hole, and move forward with our decorating plans, or we could put our plans on hold, expose all of the potential problem areas, little by little, and be sure that our basement was entirely clean! If we simply did a patch job, our basement could look beautiful much more quickly, but there may have been more mold that was unseen, and left to grow could endanger our family's health as well as the beauty of our walls in the future! The answer was clear – we must expose our walls!

We began to tear down the sheetrock. We washed down the concrete and studs with the correct solutions and used a primer to block the mold from returning. The result was a whitewashed finish! No, they weren't pristine, smooth walls, but there was a raw, clean feeling that appealed to us in a different way. It wasn't the result that we were looking for in the beginning, but new decorating possibilities opened up to us that hadn't been there before. Now that the walls were exposed, we could redirect wiring and open up spaces that before were previously boxed in. Our basement was not only getting a new look, it was getting a second chance!

That leak that we had is like sin in our lives. We may have cut out the sin and received forgiveness in that, but often sin leaves dark issues that lurk below the surface. Left to grow and unexposed those issues can damage us and our relationships. Once we discover dark places such as unforgiveness, guilt, bitterness, etc. we must decide whether we will simply patch them up, or expose them and clean out our hearts completely. If we will expose our dark places to Christ and allow Him to clean us out thoroughly, He will cover us with His love in a way that will prevent the darkness from returning. *Psalm 51:7 says, "Cleanse me with hyssop, and I will be clean; wash me, and I will be whiter than snow."*

An exposed heart may not be the look that we were going for, but a broken life mended by God is a thousand times more beautiful than a thin veneer of painted plaster that could crack at any moment! When we expose our hearts and let God clean them out, we open ourselves to new possibilities that we could have never before imagined!

God is light; in Him there is no darkness at all.
But if we walk in the light, as He is in the light, we have fellowship with one another,
and the blood of Jesus, His Son, purifies us from all sin.
1 John 1:5b, 7

Do not put out the Spirit's fire.
1 Thessalonians 5:19

Because of the increase of wickedness,
the love of most will grow cold,
but he who stands firm to the end will be saved.
Matthew 24:12

The Warmth of God's Love

At this moment, our house is very cold! We have radiant heat which runs off of an oil furnace and we accidentally let the oil run too low. Because it is the weekend, we will have to wait a few days until the oil can be delivered and then our house will be warm again! In the meantime, we have a wood-burning fireplace and we have built a roaring fire in it. Unfortunately, in a fireplace, most of the heat goes up and not out, so in order to feel the warmth of the fire we must stay very close to it. If we walk just a few steps away the coldness of the house envelopes us once more.

In the Bible, oil is a symbol of the Holy Spirit. This world that we live in has let its "oil" run dangerously low. It has become a cold place, offering very little of God's love and the warmth of Christian fellowship. In order to find the comfort that His love offers, we must stay very close to the source of the fire that lights up our spirit. God's truth and love is the only thing that can truly warm our souls. When we stay connected to the church, the fellowship of believers, and the truth of God's Word, then and only then will we be able to stay warm. If we take only a few steps away, we find that we are surrounded once again by the coldness of the world.

God teaches us in His Word that we need each other. We must join together regularly with other believers for encouragement, fellowship, discipleship, support, love, and every other thing that keeps us going. True, we are to live in the world. We must wrap ourselves in the clothes of righteousness, put on the warmth of Christ's love and step out into the cold, hard world. We are to bring light and warmth wherever we go, but we must frequently return to the glow of the fire to be warmed again and again!

It is but a short time until Christ returns. It will be a glorious day when we are continuously warmed by the physical presence of our God. When we reach Heaven we will never again have to worry about the oil running low or the warmth of our home. Until then, let us stay warm in His presence by staying close to the fire of the fellowship of other believers and continue to welcome those whom have not yet felt His warmth.

Let us not give up meeting together, as some are in the habit of doing, but let us encourage one another—and all the more as you see the Day approaching.
Hebrews 10:25

"But I will restore you to health
and heal your wounds,"
declares the Lord.
Jeremiah 30:17

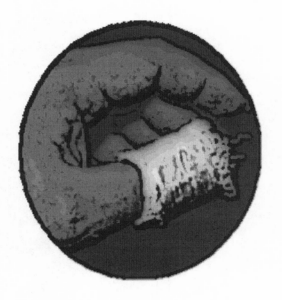

Nothing in all creation is hidden from God's sight.
Everything is uncovered
and laid bare before the eyes
of him to whom we must give account.
Hebrews 4:13

The Wounded Thumb

The other day, as I was grating an apple for muffins, I ran my thumb across the grater. Oh, it really hurt! I grabbed a wet paper towel and applied pressure while trying not to say the words that I shouldn't. I really needed to finish my baking so I bandaged it up and kept on working. Later that day, I had my friend apply a more sufficient bandage. The tight wrap kept it from hurting as badly and I liked the protection it offered. It was a painful wound but as long as I kept it wrapped up; I didn't need to worry about it.

.   Several days later, the bandage was still on my thumb. I knew I needed to unwrap it and air it out, but it felt so safe to keep it wrapped up. I knew that air on the open wound would sting and while it was covered I didn't have to see it. I was also afraid that it could get infected and maybe even get worse.

After some advice from several people, I finally did remove the bandage. The wound still appeared fresh, and just as I suspected, the air made it sting. It was nasty looking and it made me cringe just to look at it. However, after a little while it wasn't so bad and in a few days it scabbed over. Now, there is just a scar left, a reminder that while it was painful, I did survive!

Many of us do the same thing with an emotional wound. After being hurt, we wrap it up tight and nurse it quietly. If we keep it covered and bound tightly we feel more secure. After all, if we open it up, the air may make it sting and it could even get worse. There is some benefit in drawing in for a time, but the time for healing comes soon. When we keep our emotional wounds under wrap they stay fresh and will not begin to heal.

Often, we keep the wound bound up so that we do not have to see it. When we are hurt by people or circumstances, it is easier not to look. Removing our bandages causes us to admit the truth about what happened which is sometimes more painful than the wound itself.

We must learn to find a safe place where we can remove the bandages and expose the hurt. The breath of the Holy Spirit can breathe on our wounds and allow them to scab over. Once we heal, all that will be left is the scar to remind us that we have endured the pain and we have survived! A trusted friend, counselor, or pastor is a good place to begin. Though it may actually feel worse to open up, the work that is being done is important.

A wound kept under wraps will never fully heal. Allow the Great Physician to do His work. It is time to take off the bandages!

For this people's heart has become calloused; they hardly hear with their ears,
and they have closed their eyes. Otherwise they might see with their eyes,
hear with their ears, understand with their hearts and turn, and I would heal them.
Matthew 13:15

Greet one another with a kiss of love.
Peace to all of you who are in Christ.
1Peter 5:14

If you have any encouragement
from being united with Christ,
if any comfort from his love,
if any fellowship with the Spirit,
if any tenderness and compassion,
then make my joy complete by being
like-minded, having the same love,
being one in spirit and purpose.
Philippians 2:1-2

Fellowship

My husband, Jerry, and I went for a motorcycle ride the other day and I noticed an interesting thing that amazed me. Every time we passed another rider, Jerry would put his hand out to wave and the other rider would also put his hand out. We didn't know the other riders, they may have had nothing else in common with us, but there seemed to be a fellowship between those riding motorcycles. I found this very odd. We also drive a minivan, but I never wave at someone else on the road because they are also in a minivan. What is it about a motorcycle that brings about a feeling of kinship?

Perhaps it is the fact that a rider has made a special choice to be on a motorcycle. Riding a bike requires an effort and some sacrifice. A special license must be acquired and some additional training is helpful. There is gear that is specific to riding and those who ride seem to enjoy being with other riders. A motorcycle seems to be more than a mode of transportation; instead, it is a statement of identity and lifestyle. Riding a motorcycle is also somewhat controversial, so a rider must be strong in their convictions of preference.

Perhaps this is why Christian fellowship is also strong and somewhat fascinating. A person could come from any walk of life, any race, any family background, any education, any career, but because this person is a Christian, they are accepted into the family of faith. If a Christian finds himself in a primarily non-Christian atmosphere and stumbles upon another Christian, there is an instant feeling of familiarity and bonding. No other kinship, not even blood relation in some cases, promotes this kind of fellowship. There is a bond of beliefs, love, and understanding.

Shall we be like minivan drivers or motorcycle riders? We should learn to quickly recognize one another and throw up the hand of fellowship. In a culture of conformity and constantly moving traffic, it is comforting to know that there are those driving through who are also making a special choice to sacrifice and state their identity in Christ. They are the ones who are riding in freedom, strong in their convictions, and full of love for their fellow journeymen.

Let us stand out in the crowd today. Let us wear the gear that separates us from the others. Let us fully clothe ourselves in Christ and make it known that we are Christians. Let us wave to one another and join together in fellowship. Let us welcome all of those who want to join us and ride in a way that others will seek to live like us!

But if we walk in the light, as he is in the light,
we have fellowship with one another,
and the blood of Jesus, His Son, purifies us from all sin.
1 John 1:7

The creation waits in eager expectation
for the sons of God to be revealed.
Romans 8:19

Wait for the Lord,
be strong and take heart and wait for the Lord.
Psalm 27:14

Waiting

Recently my husband had day surgery and I spent a good portion of the day in the waiting room. I always like to watch the people around me because I often learn some interesting lessons from them! This time I noticed a lady waiting for her husband. She was accompanied by her daughter, granddaughter, and her great-granddaughter. When I first saw her early in the day, she was smiling, joyful, and thoroughly enjoying her great-granddaughter. They were having happy conversation and all of them seemed young for their years. I left for a little while to visit someone else in the hospital, and when I returned I saw a different scene. The lady who had been so full of light and life earlier in the day seemed tired, old, and almost depressed. At first I thought that something must have gone wrong with her husband's surgery, but the others in her company were still jovial. I wondered what might have happened that would cause such a shift in her countenance. It occurred to me after watching for a while that waiting had just worn her out.

It is amazing in our hurried, busy lives that sitting still and waiting would exhaust us so. Have you ever had to wait for something? I am not talking about standing in the line at the grocery store (though that can be very tiresome!) or sitting in the pickup line at school. I mean, have you ever had to really wait for something? The doctor's report on a sick loved one, a wayward child to return home, a hurting marriage to be restored, financial relief during hard times; those are the kind of things that we wait for with all of our hearts. How we wait, what we do with ourselves while we wait, will determine what is left of us when the wait is over.

Psalm 37:7 says, *"Be still before the Lord and wait patiently for him."* So we are commanded to be still and wait. Does this mean that we are to do absolutely nothing? Could this mean instead, that we are to stop our constant striving to make something happen and our wriggling to get out of the difficult situation? I love the verse in James that talks about this. My Children's Living Bible puts it this way - *"Dear Brothers, is your life full of difficulties and temptations? Then be happy, for when the way is rough, your patience has a chance to grow. So let it grow, and don't try to squirm out of your problems. For when your patience is finally in full bloom, then you will be ready for anything, strong in character, full and complete."* Sometimes in my waiting I am so busy squirming that I use up all of my energy! Still, doing nothing can wear us out faster than anything! When I spend a day lying around, just getting up to go to the bathroom seems to require too much effort. I don't believe that we should allow ourselves to become lazy during our waiting times. What, then, should we be doing? We should be preparing for the blessing of what God is about to do in our lives! Therefore, prepare you minds for action; be self-controlled; set your hope fully on the grace to be given you when Jesus Christ is revealed.

What better thing to do while you are waiting than to prepare! When we are waiting to be married, we prepare for the wedding. When we are waiting to have a baby, we prepare the nursery. When we are waiting for a vacation, we prepare the things we need to pack. It is the same in our journey of life. We must prepare in advance for the blessings of God. Using our time to prepare always makes the wait seem shorter. We build upon the feeling of anticipation and we are energized instead of having our energy sapped. While we are waiting, being still before God, we can prepare by praying, reading God's word, and allowing Him to change our hearts in relationships and in our circumstances. When the time of waiting is over, we will be so ready to live in the blessings that He brings forth!

The creation waits in eager expectation
for the sons of God to be revealed.
Romans 8:19

His master replied,
"Well done, good and faithful servant!
You have been faithful with a few things;
I will put you in charge of many things.
Come and share your master's happiness!"
Matthew 25:21

Whatever you do, work at it with all your heart,
as working for the Lord, not for men,
since you know that you will receive an inheritance
from the Lord as a reward.
It is the Lord you are serving.
Colossians 3:23-24

The Faith of a Child

We have a big house and a busy life. When we are getting ready to have company over, we get really serious about cleaning up and organizing. We love to joke that when the house is getting messy it must be time to have a party so that we can get it back into shape. Seriously though, the job can sometimes be overwhelming, especially to the kids. I generally have a bigger picture and the overall goal in mind, so I like to break it down for them.

When I need my children to clean up or to complete a variety of tasks, I will gather them and send them out with one task at a time. When they return with one completed, I will offer a small reward or encouragement and send them out again. This way, they stay focused on each task at hand and do not get overwhelmed by the enormity of the big picture. They view the work as something fun, and they love the positive feedback. I enjoy their smiling faces and their little hearts that are full of the desire to please me!

Sometimes we try to be so grown up. We want God to reveal the big picture to us. When He gives us an assignment, we tend to be full of questions and doubts. I think God prefers us to have the faith of a child. He loves for us to sit at his feet and wait for Him to give us one task at a time. I believe God enjoys seeing us racing off to complete our task, carefree and full of joy. I know that He delights in giving us small rewards (blessings) or encouragements when we return to Him, breathlessly, to say we have accomplished our task! He loves our smiling faces and hearts full of the desire to please Him.

We know that God has an overall goal. He alone knows His full plan and how to accomplish it. Let's treat each day- *each moment*- this way. Let us look up to the Father to say, "What is next, Lord?" Then, let us return to Him after we have been obedient to hear him say, "Well done, good and faithful servant!"

And He said, "I tell you the truth, unless you change and become like little children, you will never enter the kingdom of heaven."
Matthew 18:3

I said, "Oh, that I had the wings of a dove!
I would fly away and be at rest"
Psalm 55:6

So then, just as you received Christ Jesus as Lord,
continue to live in Him, rooted and built up in Him,
strengthened in the faith as you were taught,
and overflowing with thankfulness.

Uprooted

I have a friend who has lived in the same house for nearly forty years. She has the most beautiful flower gardens all around her house and throughout her yard. Every once in a while, I have the privilege of visiting and she shares her plants with me. It helps her to thin out the garden and I get loads of new plants. The last time I went by, I came home with a truck load of trees, flowers, and ground cover. I wasn't able to plant them all that day since it was late when I returned home, but I got right to it the next morning. Most of the plants did well, but there were a few that were traumatized by being uprooted from the soil they had always known. I watered them faithfully, but those particular plants drooped and in a few days their foliage began to wither. My only recourse was to cut off the wilted foliage. I won't be enjoying any blooms from those plants this year but, without the dead leaves draining its energy, the plants will recover and next year they will be healthy and beautiful.

Many things can leave us with the feeling of being uprooted. Sometimes it is a physical change that we experience. Moving to a new home, a career change, empty nesting, retirement, and illness are all huge physical changes that can cause us stress. Other times, an emotional change in our lives can wreak havoc with our sense of stability. We may find that a change in family relationships, friendships, or financial status throws us off of our rocker.

The result of being uprooted is trauma to our system. We feel exhausted, emotionally bruised, uncertain, and insecure, and we may find our spirits drooping or wilted. In order to give our roots a fair chance to survive, some of our "foliage" will need to be trimmed. Drawing in for a period of time will help to preserve our souls. We must let some things go and spend that time with the Lord. When we use our energy to absorb God's truths, He will nurture our spirit. We may not have the excitement of our busy lives to enjoy but, if we take that time, our souls can recover and soon they will be healthy and beautiful.

We often like to think that we are capable of continuing with life as usual even in the face of difficult changes. Some of us even think that the world will stop turning if we step out of its spin cycle for a moment. Neither of these thoughts are truth. Life will go on, and we must rest if we want to live healthy and productive lives. Uprooted plants need to be nurtured in order to survive, and human souls need the same.

When life is tough take a rest, trim the excess, draw deeply from the Word, and rely on the Lord. The time will come when you are once again deeply rooted and capable of surviving in the heat and the drought.

Blessed is the man who does not walk in the counsel of the wicked or stand in the way of sinners or sit in the seat of mockers. But his delight is in the law of the Lord and on His law he meditates day and night. He is like a tree planted by streams of water, which yields its fruit in season and whose leaf does not wither. Whatever he does prospers.
Psalm 1:1-3

Love must be sincere.
Romans 12:9

Love is patient, love is kind.
It does not envy, it does not boast,
it is not proud. It is not rude,
it is not self-seeking, it is not easily angered,
it keeps no record of wrongs.
Love does not delight in evil
but rejoices with the truth.
It always protects, always trusts,
always hopes, always perseveres.
Love never fails.
1 Corinthians 13:4-8

Choose Love

We easily recognize some kinds of love. When I first met Jerry and fell in love, the crazy feeling in the pit of my stomach was easy to recognize. When he made me steaming mad the other day, love was not so easy to see. When my children were first born and I held their sweet sleeping bodies, love was easy to recognize. When they kept me up all night screaming over teething gums it was not so easy. My adorable puppy who follows me around and looks at me with those beautiful eyes – oh so easy to love! The same puppy that knocked over the garbage can and dragged the trash all over the carport this morning - well, I think you get the picture!

Are there people in your life that are difficult to love? Are there some that you used to love, until they disappointed you or hurt you? God urges us to love intentionally and in a sincere way. Romans 12:10 says, *"Be devoted to one another in brotherly love."* Devoted is a word that is not frequently used today. It implies a selfless love, enduring, persevering, no matter what! This verse continues to say, *"Honor one another above yourselves."* Ouch!

Love is not supposed to be a feeling. We are not to base our love for others on the warm-fuzzies (or lack there of). Instead, love is a choice and an action. We choose to love others no matter how they are behaving or how they make us feel. We must make the decision to love, no matter what.

In our humanness, we do not have the capacity for that kind of love. Only a heart that has God's Spirit of love within it can demonstrate love for the unlovely. When I spend time with the Lord, reading His Word and praying, He will renew my mind and give me the kind of love I need to pour out onto others.

Thank God that He does not base His love for me on my behavior! Just yesterday, I threw a temper tantrum, complained all day, and disobeyed a specific command that He gave me. Yet, as I talked with Him, I could feel His forgiveness and tenderness. God chooses to love me because He is Love! When I spend time in that love it transforms me into a person who can choose that kind of love for others too – even when I don't easily recognize it!

We love because He first loved us.
1 John 4:19

Many are the plans in a man's heart,
but it is the Lord's purpose that prevails.
Proverbs 19:21

For it is God who works in you to will
and to act according to His good purpose.

Just a Weed

I plopped down on the ground the other day to pout about a seemingly hope-less situation. As I ran through all of the horrible "what-if" scenarios that might crop up, I picked a weed from nearby and fiddled with it mindlessly. While I was plucking the leaves, I suddenly took notice of what I was holding. The tiny flower on this com-mon weed was no bigger than the nail on my pinky finger, but the detail in that little thing was incredible!

The flower resembled a tall, graceful goblet. The stem and cup of the bloom was a brilliant violet color, while the inside made a bowl of gleaming white. There were veins of deep purple lining the inside and proud stamen shot straight up from the stem wearing a crown of orange pollen. A hood of violet gracefully covered the bowl and the flower wore a bowtie of pale lavender with a violet dot in the center of each side. The whole delicate bud rose out of frilly dark green foliage with touches of purple and maroon. It was the most exotic flower I have ever seen! It is one of the most com-mon weeds in our yard.

I turned to my young friend, Bella, and asked her, "Why do think that God would put so much detail into a common weed?" She thought for a moment and an-swered, "Maybe to God, it isn't just a weed."

Not just a weed? That thought really got me pondering my life. If that little flower is not just a weed, if that little flower has purpose, then maybe my life has pur-pose too! Maybe even these little situations that keep cropping up in the well-planned lawn of my life are not just weeds either. Perhaps, instead of viewing them from way up high, I should stoop down and examine them more closely. Maybe I should even sit for a while and enjoy the variety and beauty that they bring to my life.

Each and every event in my life has purpose. God is in control and knows the things that will cross my path. Some are blessings; they are exciting and welcome, like a beautiful flower that bloomed at the right time. Some are lessons; they are expected and accepted, like a plant that I should have watered more often. But some of those events are more like weeds. They are annoying and bothersome, like dandelions that I just can't get rid of. They seem to crop up out of nowhere and take the place of my wonderful grass that spreads reliably across the yard. Now, though, I think I may look at them a little differently. I intend to inspect them more closely. I hope I will learn to find purpose in those events instead of looking at them as a common weed.

Not just a weed? What is cropping up in your lawn today?

And we know that all that happens to us is working for our good
if we love God and are fitting into his plans.
Romans 8:28 (Living Bible)

How can a young man keep his way pure?
By living according to your word.
Psalm 119:9

You were getting along so well.
Who has interfered with you to hold
you back from following the truth?
It certainly isn't God who has done it,
for He is the One who has called you
to freedom in Christ.
But it takes only one wrong person among
you to infect all the others.
Galatians 5:7-9

Pure Truth

When I was an art teacher, I always did a unit with the kids on painting and color. There are two types of color that we talked about. The first, primary colors include red, blue, and yellow. These colors are pure and basic; you cannot make them by mixing together any other colors. They are what they are and that will not change. Secondary colors however, are made by mixing together the primaries. You can get a wide variety of colors by mixing them, and when you blend in white or black you find even more shades and tints of those colors. It is true that blended colors seem more soothing to the eye and even appear more realistic, but we must remember that blended colors are not pure.

Truth is like color. In our world there is a lot of "blending" of truths. God's Truth, His Word, is like the primary colors. It is pure, real, and unadulterated. There is nothing else that you can mix in order to make pure Truth. Truth never changes. If you blend it with other worldly truths it is no longer truth. Truth is primary, foundational, bold, and eternal.

The world has its own set of truths. The world's truths are ever-changing. As one culture mixes with another, and one person's theories blend with others, truths shift and become less certain. How many truths have you been taught that have changed within your lifetime?

As an artist, I have become adept at mixing colors. I learned that if I blended colors and used them in a certain way; I could make a flat, two-dimensional surface appear three-dimensional and realistic. I have learned to employ a technique called Trompe l'oeil, which means to fool the eye.

Our enemy also knows this technique. He has learned to use the blending and mixing of truths to make that which is false to appear real. Blended truths take on the quality of faux depth. They fool the heart into believing that which is a lie. While the variety of truths that our society has to choose from may seem more appealing to us now, they will leave us empty and unfulfilled in the long run.

Once red has been mixed with another color, there is nothing that can be mixed with it to bring it back to pure red. The whole batch must be thrown out. There is no way to get pure red but to begin with the pigment itself.

Let's throw out the whole batch! Let us go to the source to find for ourselves what is pure and right. Let us find Truth from Truth Himself. What Truth would you prefer – the changing, blended truths of the world, or pure, unchanging Truth?

Jesus answered, "I am the way and the Truth and the life.
No one comes to the Father except through me."

And those who walk in pride,
He is able to humble.
Daniel 4:37

Humble yourself before the Lord,
and He will lift you up.
James 4:10

Trapped

When we decided to raise chickens, my husband, Jerry, built the most beautiful chicken coop in our back yard. He took great pains to make the coop secure to keep the chickens safe from predators like foxes, hawks, and mainly our dogs! The other day, I watched as the kids went out to check on the chickens. One of the children accidentally left the door open and Rover got into the coop. I ran out quickly to get him before any tragedy occurred. I had that incident in mind the next day when I went out to feed the hens. I slipped into the coop and immediately shut the door behind me. The moment I heard the latch click, I realized that there was no way to open the coop from the inside and I was home alone! I tried to wave to a neighbor on his lawn mower but he smiled and waved back, thinking I was just being friendly. I looked around desperately, but nobody else was in sight. I was contemplating my afternoon with my clucking friends when I realized suddenly that my cell phone was in my pocket! I called another neighbor and, with a chuckle, she came to rescue me from being locked in the chicken coop for the day!

The times I have found myself in an unwanted situation are more than I can count! Sometimes I get into trouble unaware of the danger of the situation, and sometimes it is because of a bad decision I have made. Regardless of the reason, once I get in, it is sometimes hard to see a way out. When I am tempted, it is a bit like being locked in or trapped. The enemy would like me to feel that I am *in it for the day* so I may as well enjoy myself. I may even try a half-hearted plea of help to someone who is really not in a position to offer it. However, God tells us in His word that we are never really trapped and that He always provides a way out!

Often, when we are stuck in sin or trouble of any kind, it is embarrassing to have to ask for help. The way out that God provides for us is seldom an easy choice to make. I didn't like having to call my neighbor and admit that I had locked myself in the chicken coop; however, the alternative was not pleasant either. Pride is usually the very thing that keeps us locked in. We would prefer to stay stuck in a situation that we know is not good than to ask another person to bail us out.

Humility is that key that unlocks the door of sin's trap. Once we confess that we are unable to help ourselves, we make room for God's provision. He will not delay in his rescue, but we must let go of our pride, humble ourselves, and admit to God that we are stuck. Don't let the enemy talk you into spending the day in the coop, help is only a call away!

No temptation has seized you except what is common to man. And God is faithful;
He will not let you be tempted beyond what you can bear. But when you are tempted,
He will also provide a way out so that you can stand up under it.
1 Corinthians 10:13

The Lord is compassionate and gracious,
slow to anger, abounding in love.
Psalm 103:8

Have mercy on me, O God, according to your
unfailing love; according to your great compassion
blot out my transgressions.
Psalm 51:1

Rose-colored Glasses

Some days my children exhaust me! Last Monday was one of those days. It seemed that I spent the day cleaning up their messes, breaking up their fights, kissing their hurts, and serving their many demands. It was a day of fussing, whining, complaining, and not the best of behavior. By the time I got them to bed, I was rethinking the whole parenting thing! Once they quieted down and drifted off to sleep I finally had a few moments to catch my breath and unwind. Before I went to bed, I peeked in to check on them. What sweet children! They were peaceful, even angelic in their slumber and suddenly it was difficult to remember the troubles of the day. How could I stay angry and frustrated with such darling little ones?

This morning, as I got up early to walk, the sky was pink with the rising sun and the whole world seemed softer and sweeter. I wonder if some days feel to God like my days have felt. Days filled with fussing, complaining children. When He has days spent cleaning up our messes, breaking up our fights, kissing our hurts, and serving our many demands, does He ever feel frustrated over our whining and lack of good behavior? Do you think He peeks in on us in the wee hours of the morning through the rosy glow of the sunrise to see us while we are peaceful? When He sees us as we were made to be; quiet, still, untouched by the troubles of the world, does He wonder, "How could I remain angry with them?"

I am so grateful for a Heavenly Father who is able to love me despite my behavior during the day. How awesome that He sees me through His "rose-colored" glasses with new compassion every morning!

Because of the Lord's great love we are not consumed,
for His compassions never fail.
They are new every morning;
great is your faithfulness.
Lamentations 3:22-23

Wendy Custer is the founder of W3 Vision Ministries
(Worship and Wisdom for Women), a non-denominational
para church ministry dedicated to the encouragement of women.

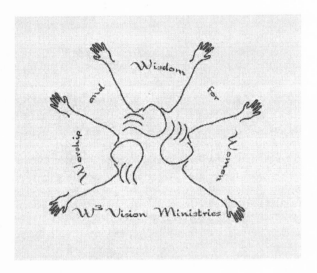

Visit their website at www.freewebs.com/w3vision/ Subscribers to
the website receive a free "Cup of Encouragement" weekly by email.